PR

Transforming Your Thought ...

"Amazing book! Like a detailed map, this book leads teens out of the pits of unhealthy thinking and into the fields of freedom that come with a renewed mind! Sarah has created a biblically-solid, wise, and authentic journey to help young women examine their thought lives. It's practical. It's inspirational. It's encouraging. Young women must be prepared for the life-long thought battle that will happen inside their heads. This book equips them to win."

—Heather Creekmore, author of
Compared to Who? and *The Burden of Better*

"I wish I could give every teen girl a copy of Sarah's phenomenal book, but it was with deep gratitude that I placed it in the hands of my own teen daughter. The deeply grooved habits of our inner thought lives are laid down in adolescence. Sarah's book is a much-needed guide for developing patterns of thought that are life-giving rather than life-destroying. Practical, accessible, and beautifully personal, *Transforming Your Thought Life* is a treasure."

—Christie Purifoy, author of *Roots and Sky* and *Placemaker*

"This book is a must-read for all women, especially teen girls who are battling toxic thoughts. Sarah uses personal stories and practical tools to help lead readers on a journey to transform their thought life and center on biblical truth. I especially appreciated the reflection questions and relatable stories she includes to illuminate each chapter."

—Dorina Lazo Gilmore-Young, author of *Walk Run Soar*,
speaker, podcaster, and mother of three girls

"In *Transforming Your Thought Life for Teens*, Sarah reaches teens right where they are at. Recognizing the various ways our thoughts hold them captive and steal their peace. I can't think of a better time, when we see depression on the rise to help them see the battle of the mind as something that can be won."

—Gena McCown, author of *Women's Ministry with Purpose*

"I loved reading this book with my two middle-school-aged daughters! This powerful resource is packed with practical and biblical ways to deal with negative emotions, destructive thoughts, and painful experiences. *Transforming Your Thought Life for Teens* sheds light on why young girls struggle with negative thoughts and offers useful tools to help them focus on God's Truth instead. My girls enjoyed the personal stories in each chapter, and the reflection questions opened up new avenues of conversation for our family. This book equips teens who struggle with their identity, emotions, and friendships to 'take captive every thought to make it obedient to Christ (2 Cor. 10:5).'"

—Sarah Koontz, Bible Study Author
and Founder of Living by Design Ministries

"Of the many benefits of following Jesus, today's girl may just need His peace most of all. In *Transforming Your Thought Life,* Sarah Geringer helps girls find God's power available to them at all times in all settings as they set their thoughts intentionally on the Lord. A powerful resource!"

—Lynn Cowell, author of *Brave Beauty* &
Loved & Cherished: 100 Devotions for Girls

"Fully relatable and founded firmly on Scripture, Sarah offers teen girls hope and freedom in *Transforming Your Thought Life for Teens*. As I read her stories and walked through her exercises, I found myself thinking about the teen version of who I was and wishing I had something like this to help me. It offers both help for the struggles girls face as well as the opportunity to prevent those struggles from becoming lifelong battles. Deeper than a quick devotional, *Transforming Your Thought Life for Teens* offers girls a chance to interact with God's Word to set up a strong foundation for a faith they can walk out as they become adults. I look forward to sharing this with my own teen daughters!"

—Rebecca Hastings, author of
Daily Meditations for Christians

"In our counseling offices, we see the difference that a daily practice of Christian medication can make in a teen girl's mental health. As I speak with girls both face-to-face and in assemblies across the country, one thing they all say they struggle with is self-worth and the negative thoughts they have about themselves. *Transforming Your Thought Life for Teens* provides practical suggestions and Scriptures that girls can use on a daily basis to retrain their brains. I'm excited to add this resource to our counseling center library."

—Michelle Nietert, M.A., LPC-S, clinical director,
Community Counseling Associates;
National Mental Health Expert;
and author of *Loved and Cherished*

"Sarah does a masterful job of exploring the various thoughts that teens struggle with, relating to the reader in a very personal, honest, and transparent style. Guiding the teen reader to consider their thought life is a challenging endeavor, but Sarah's approach helps the reader to feel accepted, not condemned. Thoughts are able to be viewed in light of Scripture with gently guided reflection questions that help the reader to come to their own conclusions."

—Denise Pass, author of *Make Up Your Mind* and *Shame Off You*, founder of Seeing Deep Ministries

TRANSFORMING
Your
THOUGHT
LIFE
for Teens

TRANSFORMING *Your* THOUGHT LIFE *for Teens*

RENEW YOUR MIND WITH GOD

SARAH GERINGER

LEAFWOOD
PUBLISHERS
an imprint of Abilene Christian University Press

Transforming Your Thought Life for Teens
Renew Your Mind with God

LEAFWOOD
P U B L I S H E R S
an imprint of Abilene Christian University Press

Copyright © 2021 by Sarah Geringer
ISBN 978-1-68426-221-2
Printed in the United States of America

Scripture quotations, unless otherwise noted, are from The Holy Bible, New International Version®, NIV®. Copyright © 1973, 1978, 1984, 2011 by Biblica, Inc.® Used by permission. All rights reserved worldwide.

Scripture quotations are from the ESV® Bible (The Holy Bible, English Standard Version®), copyright © 2001 by Crossway, a publishing ministry of Good News Publishers. Used by permission. All rights reserved.

Scripture quotations marked NLT are taken from the New Living Translation, Copyright ©1996, 2004, 2007 by Tyndale House Foundation. Used by permission of Tyndale House Publishers, Inc., Carol Stream, IL 60188. All rights reserved.

Scripture quotations marked NRSV are from the Revised Standard Version of the Bible, copyright © 1946, 1952, and 1971 National Council of the Churches of Christ in the United States of America. Used by permission. All rights reserved worldwide.

Scriptures noted NKJV are taken from the New King James Version® Copyright © 1982 by Thomas Nelson. Used by permission. All rights reserved.

Published in Association with WordWise Media Services

Library of Congress Cataloging-in-Publication Data

Names: Geringer, Sarah, 1977– author.
Title: Transforming your thought life for teens : renew your mind with God / Sarah Geringer.
Identifiers: LCCN 2021014963 (print) | LCCN 2021014964 (ebook) | ISBN 9781684262212 (trade paperback) | ISBN 9781684269181 (ebook)
Subjects: LCSH: Thought and thinking—Religious aspects—Christianity. | Meditation—Christianity. | Teenagers—Religious life.
Classification: LCC BV4598.4 .G47 2021 (print) | LCC BV4598.4 (ebook) | DDC 248.83—dc23
LC record available at https://lccn.loc.gov/2021014963
LC ebook record available at https://lccn.loc.gov/2021014964

Cover design by Thinkpen Design
Interior text design by Scribe Inc.

Leafwood Publishers is an imprint of Abilene Christian University Press
ACU Box 29138
Abilene, Texas 79699
1-877-816-4455
www.leafwoodpublishers.com

21 22 23 24 25 26 / 7 6 5 4 3 2 1

For Lauren

Colossians 2:6–7

CONTENTS

Acknowledgments

First and foremost, I thank God for working all things together for my good to produce this book. You had this book in mind when you told me at age sixteen, in the darkest valleys of my life, that I would be a writer. Thank you for creating me to be a wounded healer who helps others find a voice for their pain and then seeks freedom in you.

I thank my husband, Derrick, and my children, Drake, Ethan, and Lauren, for supporting me in my writing ministry. Your encouragement and practical help in my book creation seasons are essential, and I love you all.

Thank you to the members of my launch team for *Transforming Your Thought Life: Christian Meditation in Focus,* who inspired this idea. Several of you shared my book with your teenage daughters and told me it was so helpful to them. You are the first ones who asked me to write a book specifically for Gen Z girls. Without your input, I would not have considered writing it. Your inspiration and support have been priceless.

Thank you to the hardworking team at Leafwood Publishers, who welcomed this book idea with open arms. It's a joy to work with you again!

Thank you to Michelle S. Lazurek of WordWise Media Services. Your gifts as an agent continue to bless me, and I can't wait to see what God has in store for both of us.

Thank you to all my readers and online followers. It is a privilege to serve you, which I don't take for granted. May this book be a blessing to a new harvest field.

Soli Deo Gloria

How Christian Meditation Transforms Your Thoughts

I have rejoiced in your laws as much as in riches.
I will study your commandments and reflect on your
ways.
I will delight in your decrees and not forget your word.
Psalm 119:14–16 NLT

I walked through the junior high hallway, wanting to blend in. I looked down, trying to avoid attention from the kids I didn't know at this much bigger public school. I missed my small, familiar private Christian school and didn't understand how to step on the social ladder, much less climb it. So I tried to not stand out or attract any stares.

Yet I heard the slightest whispers. Two girls turned their heads toward each other in private conversation, and then both looked back at me. I wish they had offered me open, friendly smiles. But their smiles were smirks instead. I didn't hear what they had said, but it had to be something in mean-girl language. About me.

It wasn't even 8:00 A.M., but my day felt ruined. What had I done? Why couldn't they leave me alone? Hot tears pressed at my eyes. Just in time, I reached my locker and opened the door, using it as a shield. I blinked back the tears while sticking my face in as if looking for something. I wished I could have crawled inside to not face the day.

At that time, I was a Bible-believing church girl. I had memorized over one hundred Bible verses in preparation for my confirmation just a few months before. But I had yet to realize my potential to unlock the power of those verses with Christian meditation. I could have chosen just one of them as a shield instead of my locker door. Satan was trying to defeat me through the girls' whispers, which may not have been about me anyway.

I wish I had written Philippians 4:13 on the cover of my notebook and glanced at it the first moment I felt insecure: "I can do all this through him who gives me strength." I could have repeated it silently in my mind, focusing on the truth of God's Word rather than my feelings. Then I could have made it into a quick prayer: "God, help me walk through this hallway in your strength." Once at my locker, I could have whispered the verse to myself and then continued in prayer: "Help me get through this entire day in your strength, Lord." What a difference that approach would have made!

If you're reading this book, you may have grown up like me. You know the Bible stories, you've heard the sermons, and you've been to church camp. Yet you may not understand the ability you already possess to transform your thought life. And you may not realize that Satan is opposing you in your thoughts, trying to take you down where the problems begin. By the way, if you didn't have those faith experiences growing up, you are in a perfect place to start renewing your mind by meditating on the Bible.

This book will help you learn how to replace the lies you believe from Satan, yourself, and others with the truth of God's Word. You won't simply empty your mind to fill it up with feel-good memes. You will renew your mind—make it new—with the Holy Spirit's help. You can have peace, joy, and confidence that last when you intentionally hide God's Word in your heart and mind through Christian meditation.

❀ WHAT IS CHRISTIAN MEDITATION?

Does that word *meditation* sound foreign to you? Perhaps you envision someone sitting with legs crossed on the floor, hands in a prayer pose, and eyes closed as they mumble "Mmmmm." But Christian meditation is nothing like that. It is simply thinking deeply about Scripture. It's taking a few deliberate steps to help those verses stick in your mind, so your thoughts can be transformed in just a few minutes every day.

The word *meditate* is used up to twenty times in the Bible, depending on the version you use. In Hebrew, the terms *hagah* and *siach* are the primary words for meditation.

In Isaiah 31:4, *hagah* is used to describe a lion who "growls" over his prey. Though shepherds circle the lion and try to frighten it with loud noises, the lion is highly focused and will not move away. He is centered on his purpose of conquering and devouring his meal. In another chapter, Isaiah uses *hagah* as a picture of mourning doves "moaning" to demonstrate how King Hezekiah cried out for God's help during a terminal illness (Isa. 38:14). A dove's cry is repetitive and based on instinct, which is key to its calling as a bird in God's creation.

Your time of meditation may or may not be vocal. But it can be natural, centered, focused, and repetitive like the animal sounds Isaiah used as metaphors. With practice and memory, your experience of Christian meditation will become more intentional.

The word *siach* is used many times in the Psalms to describe undistracted and concentrated thinking. The psalmist uses *siach* eight different times in Psalm 119 to describe different times to meditate on God's precepts, both day and night (119:15, 23, 27, 48, 78, 97, 99, 148). Sometimes *siach* is used to describe deep feelings of anguish or complaint, as in Psalm 142:2 and Proverbs 23:29. Our times of meditation are not dry and boring. They are invitations to share our hearts with God as we focus on him and cry out in authenticity.

Christian meditation isn't fuzzy and weird. Nor is it cold and distant. It involves the solid truth of God's Word, plus our thoughts, feelings, and experiences. It's an invitation to a deeper relationship with the One who perfectly loves us. When we focus on God's character, promises, teachings, and works, we engage in Christian meditation.

❀ THE BENEFITS OF CHRISTIAN MEDITATION

Can you believe that you have around 60,000 thoughts every day? That's an average of 2,500 thoughts every hour and about 42 thoughts every minute. For most of us, nearly all of those thoughts are negative and are recycled from yesterday's thoughts.[1] However, you can replace those negative thoughts with Scripture truths, so you have a renewed thought life.

Christian meditation has transformed the way I think. When I was a young woman, I challenged myself to read through the entire Bible, cover to cover, for the first time. I bought a One Year Bible, which divides the Scripture into daily readings. That edition had one verse in bold every day, which I used for daily meditation. Within a few weeks of practicing this, I noticed I had greater peace in every area of my life. It can do the same for you. Here are other benefits you can experience through Christian meditation.

SPIRITUAL BENEFITS

Take a few minutes to read the first chapter of the book of Job. You will see that Satan used Job's life as a battlefield between him and God. Satan also uses your mind as a battlefield. When you meditate on Scripture, you will have spiritual weapons to fight back against your enemy, Satan.

MENTAL BENEFITS

Scientists have proven that you can increase your concentration and improve your memory skills through meditation.[2] Christian meditation may help you build better study habits for school. But even better than that, it helps you pull out God's Word right when you need it. You don't even need a physical Bible or a Bible app when God's Word is hidden in your mind through meditation.

PHYSICAL BENEFITS

Christian meditation is a great way to deal with stress. When you regularly meditate on God's Word, you can lower your blood pressure and stress-hormone levels.[3] Your body produces cortisol when you are stressed. This stress hormone can cause you to eat more because you feel hungrier. As you reduce cortisol levels through meditation, you can have fewer food cravings, a stronger immune system to fight off diseases, and better sleep.

EMOTIONAL BENEFITS

Almost every girl feels self-conscious about her body image and worth, which can cause a range of tough emotions. As you meditate on God's Word and learn how he sees you, you can start seeing yourself with healthier emotions and build your confidence. If you have difficulties in your relationships, meditating on the truths in God's Word can help you heal from hurt.

SOCIAL BENEFITS

When you think about the type of life God wants you to live, you will become a healthier and happier daughter, sister, friend, relative, student, and worker. The Holy Spirit wants to bear the fruit of self-control in you (Gal. 5:22–23), and by practicing meditation, you can develop self-control. It will help you think before you speak in social situations, which can improve your relationships with family, friends, and boys. Christian meditation will also help you be prepared to share your faith with others.

✻ HOW TO PRACTICE CHRISTIAN MEDITATION

When I meditate on a certain Scripture, I ask myself three questions:

1. What does this verse tell me about God?
2. What does this verse tell me about the life God wants me to live?
3. What does this verse tell me about how God wants me to serve others?

You can use this technique on any passage of God's Word. Let's try it with the theme Scripture for this chapter. Practice reading the verse slowly and thoughtfully at least three times before reading the words below it. Then write the Scripture out to help seal it in your memory. I'll guide you through each verse, and then feel free to add your own thoughts in the blanks.

> *I have rejoiced in your laws as much*
> *as in riches. (Ps. 119:14)*

If you could have everything you wanted, what would be on your list? I'd love to have an all-expenses-paid, two-week trip to France. It's fun to dream like that. But God wants our hearts set on him more than all the riches in the world. He knows that if we put him first, we will be happier and more satisfied.

Write the verse:

_____

_____

_____

_____

_____

Your thoughts:

_____

_____

_____

_____

_____

> *I will study your commandments and*
> *reflect on your ways. (Ps. 119:15)*

What is the most important test you've ever taken? Maybe it was a science, math, or English final, or perhaps a standardized test for college prep. Have you ever studied God's Word with that same type of intensity? You can study God's commands out of respect for him. It's also helpful to reflect on God's ways, which are higher than ours (Isa. 55:9). When we reflect on God's ways, we get to know him on a deeper level.

Write the verse:

_____

_____

_____

_____

_____

Your thoughts:

_____

_____

_____

_____

_____

> *I will delight in your decrees and not*
> *forget your word. (Ps. 119:16)*

What delights you? I take delight in my Labrador retriever, fresh flowers, and Krispy Kreme donuts. God wants us to delight in his decrees, or statements, just like we delight in our favorite things. He wants us to take steps to remember his Word and not forget it because it is so important. I will give you some easy tips on how to do this in the next section.

Write the verse:

_____

_____

_____

_____

_____

Your thoughts:

_____

_____

_____

_____

_____

Congratulations! You have just completed your first Christian meditation exercise. See how quick and easy it is to get God's Word into your heart and mind? Here are more tips on how to help God's Word take hold through Christian meditation.

1. Make it a habit. In your morning routine, you probably have several habits in place, like brushing your teeth and putting on your shoes. You do these things without thinking because you've practiced them so many times. To get the maximum benefits from Christian meditation, you'll need to develop a habit. Commit to working through this book for the next twenty-one days, and you'll be on your way to getting that habit in place.

2. Choose a good time for meditation. You only need a few minutes each day. You can meditate in the shower or bath, while performing chores, during exercise, or right before you go to sleep. Maybe you could give up fifteen minutes of time on social media for Christian meditation. It doesn't matter when meditation happens as long as you make time for it.

3. Find a quiet spot. Since your own mind will try to distract you when you are meditating, you'll need to go somewhere quiet to cut down on all other noises. Do you have noise-canceling headphones? They are a great tool for Christian meditation. If you don't have your own bedroom, you could try the bathroom or even a closet.

4. Bring your Bible. You can use a printed Bible, a Bible app, or a Scripture verse on a note or card. I like to search biblegateway .com for topics and meditate on several verses on a theme. You could use a single verse of Psalms or Proverbs every day for meditation. The possibilities are endless as long as a Bible passage is the main focus.

5. Start with prayer. Simply ask God to quiet your mind so you can focus on his Word. Ask him to help you understand the passage and apply it. One of the Holy Spirit's main jobs is to teach you the truth from the Word (John 14:26). As you ask God for help, he will surely provide for you.

6. Repeat the words. Speak the verse slowly several times, pausing on different words each time for different emphasis. Try to consider the meaning of each word as you say it, which will help you gain the maximum benefit from the verse.

7. Ask questions. The three questions I previously mentioned can help you understand the verse even more. You can also ask more questions specific to the verse. Ask your parents, teachers, youth leaders, or pastor for help if you don't understand a verse.

8. Write it out. Keep one notebook or binder for your meditation times, where you can write out the verse and record what you have learned. By writing out the verse, you have a much better chance of remembering it.[4] Every month or so, review your notes. I use my notes as research material for my books; who knows how God will use your notes in the future?

9. End with prayer. Thank God for what he has taught you. Praise him for what you learned about him. Ask him to help you apply the verse to your life. Also, ask him if he wants you to put the verse in action for someone else, or simply share it with them.

10. Post your verse. To help you remember your verse, post it somewhere you will see it often. Jot it on a sticky note and place it on your bathroom mirror, student planner, or laptop computer. You can also make the verse a screensaver on your phone. All these methods will help you hide God's Word in your memory.

Now that you know the basics of Christian meditation, you're ready to get started on this twenty-one-day thought life transformation journey. In the following chapters, we will look at common thought life problem areas for teen girls. We will look at specific verses you can use to take control of your thoughts and increase your peace. You'll find many Bible verses mentioned in the following chapters. I suggest having your Bible open along with a notebook to look them up and write them down as you go. Let's start this journey together in prayer.

Prayer

Heavenly Father,

I praise you because you are my God. I want to honor you with my thoughts. My mind belongs to you. I want my thoughts to look more like yours, starting today.

I confess that my thoughts are often a mess. Too many times, my thoughts are stuck in the junk of this world. I can't change my thoughts myself, Lord. I need your help. Renew me from the inside out.

Thank you for leading me on this renewal journey. I am thankful that the Holy Spirit lives in me, and you will help me make needed changes.

Guide me in the days ahead. Remind me to schedule time every day to meditate on your Word. I ask for courage and strength to win the battle in my thought life. Give me the mind of Christ as I start on this path of renewal.

In Jesus's name,

Amen.

REFLECTION QUESTIONS

1. What new concept did you learn about Christian meditation?

2. Which area of your life—spiritual, mental, emotional, physical, or social—could benefit the most from Christian meditation in the next twenty-one days?

3. What is the best time of day for you to meditate on God's Word?

ONE

CARELESS THOUGHTS

We take captive every thought to make it obedient to Christ.

2 Corinthians 10:5

In third grade, I received a "gift" from a cute, popular boy in my class. After a round of playful teasing, he gave me an honest compliment. My cheeks turned bright red—even though I couldn't see them, they felt hot, and I knew they were glowing with embarrassment. But that night, in the quiet of my bedroom, I could replay that moment without distraction and the fear of anyone watching.

Little did I know that the third-grade incident would turn into a thirty-year thought life struggle. It turned into an attempt to escape through daydreams. Nothing more risqué than a Hallmark movie, where the girl always ends up with the boy of her dreams. But this carelessness with my thought life affected me all through high school, college, and yes, even my marriage.

If we fail to control our thoughts, the careless treatment can create deep ruts in our brains. Mine was a rut of escape when I felt stressed, sad, or lonely. Yours could be a rut for anger, guilt, fear, or other negative emotions. Since your thoughts contain seeds for words and actions, it's essential to learn how to examine them when you're young, so you can be more intentional with what you say and do for years to come.

However, God gave us females the special ability to jump from subject to subject in our brains. One husband and wife author team compared female thoughts to spaghetti, which loops around and around itself. They compared male thoughts to waffles, with separate boxes for individual categories.[1] If your dad, brother, or male friend has ever said to you, "Can you just get to the point?" they may have been feeling lost in your slide from noodle to noodle.

If all our thought noodles were good, there would be no need for this book. Of course, you and I know some of those thought noodles are negative. Take a slide down those negative noodles, and you could end up in a bad place fast. Those are the types of thoughts we can fix through Christian meditation.

To renew your mind, you need to examine all types of thoughts, not just the good ones. It's kind of like looking in the bottom of your purse or book bag when you clean it out. Let's take a look at the random things I found in my purse:

- a pair of earrings
- an empty plastic bottle of hand sanitizer
- expired coupons
- a pen that has run dry
- receipts that need to be filed
- a used tissue—yuck!

Items like these represent my careless thoughts. Some thoughts are out of place, like my earrings. Others can be recycled into something better, like the plastic bottle. Some thoughts aren't useful anymore, like the expired coupons and dry pen. Several thoughts need to be filed away for future use. I need to throw a few disgusting thoughts away right now, like the used tissue.

If we all have careless thoughts, why don't we tend to them? It's because no one else sees them, just like no one looks into the bottom of your purse or book bag. Except God. He sees the messy thoughts we try to hide from everyone else and wants to help us examine them.

Examining your thoughts is called *metacognition*, or thinking about thinking. To begin the mind renewal process, we'll look at many categories of thoughts. The unifying factor is that these thoughts are careless, or unexamined. To have a renewed mind, you must think about the quality of your thoughts.

❋ THE FIGHT TO RENEW YOUR MIND

When you start out to renew your mind, it won't be easy. It's better if you expect a fight on three different fronts. You'll fight yourself, Satan, and others.

FIGHTING YOURSELF

Have you ever tried to eat healthier or start an exercise program? Your own willpower might get you through day two, but then your resolve caves. This is because "the spirit is willing, but the flesh is weak" (Matt. 26:41). You are literally at war with yourself, trying to choose between good and evil. The apostle Paul writes about this struggle in Romans 7:15–25. Often we are our own worst enemies in our thought lives.

However, you can renew your mind by meditating on Scripture. The verses you study will serve as shields in your thought life. God wants to help you fight your own tendencies toward sin through the power of his Word.

FIGHTING YOUR ENEMY

Every minute of every day, Satan is looking for you to slip up in your thought life so he can take advantage of your weaknesses. Now that you're reading this book and working on a renewal process, expect him to double down on his efforts. He sees your mind as a battlefield where he wages war against you. Ephesians 6:12 tells us, "For our struggle is not against flesh and blood, but against the rulers, against the authorities, against the powers of this dark world and against the spiritual forces of evil in the heavenly realms."

Satan often shoots flaming arrows of ugliness, hate, and condemnation into your mind's battlefield. Your unexamined thoughts are like tinder, perfect for starting fires. If you don't extinguish them right away with the life-giving water of God's truth, wildfire can blaze through your camp.

Have you ever struggled with a thought life problem that just wouldn't quit? That could be a stronghold set up by Satan. A stronghold is where Satan gets a hook in and starts building a mini power base. You can remove a spiritual stronghold only with God's help.

FIGHTING OTHERS

If you've ever been the recipient of unloving words, you understand the power harsh words have to hurt you. Sometimes it's the hurtful silence of others that speaks louder than words. Negative expressions from other people can create landmines in our minds' battlefields.

Growing up, I heard a lot of critical words about my weight. Some words were mean and ugly, spoken by rude kids who picked on me. Others were well-intended words spoken by loved ones, yet they wounded me deep inside. These criticisms infiltrated my thinking about my body image for many years, which created a heavier load than I was meant to bear.

If other people are saying or doing things that are holding you back from thought life renewal, God can set you free from these burdens. He can give you the freedom and hope you're seeking. Let's look at a Scripture verse that can help us choose these virtues.

❄ MEDITATING ON GOD'S WORD

Romans 8:6 states, "The mind governed by the flesh is death, but the mind governed by the Spirit is life and peace." I'll guide you through a meditation on this verse.

The mind governed

At any given moment, your mind is governed, or ruled, by positive or negative thoughts. Stop for a moment and read Job 1:6–12. You can see the spiritual battle in this story. In your mind as well, your healthy thoughts please God, and your unhealthy thoughts please Satan.

by the flesh

Our flesh is our sinful human nature. My sinful human nature always moves toward what is easy, painless, and lazy. The root of flesh-based thoughts is selfishness. Most of my unchecked thoughts follow that self-centered path. But I don't want my thoughts to be governed by my flesh. I know you want renewal just like I do.

is death

Unhealthy thoughts always lead to a kind of death. For example, years of negative thoughts about my weight led to my believing lies that made relationships impossible. Left unchecked, unhealthy thoughts can lead to literal death too. For total renewal, we must surrender our thoughts to God's transforming work. If not, we are headed down a slippery slope to death.

but the mind governed by the Spirit

We have a choice—submit to the Holy Spirit's rule, or fall to the power of ourselves, Satan, and others. The Holy Spirit's rules are like ones from a loving parent, rules that protect us and offer us the best possible life. When we willingly surrender to the Holy Spirit's rule in our thoughts, we will experience greater blessings.

is life and peace.

The best life and perfect peace are possible, even abundant, through the Holy Spirit's rule. In his power, we can destroy Satan's strongholds, conquer the war between spirit and flesh, and avoid death by submitting our thoughts to him.

Write the verse:

_____
_____
_____
_____
_____

Your thoughts:

_____
_____
_____
_____
_____

✤ OBEDIENCE WITH THE HOLY SPIRIT'S HELP

The Holy Spirit is the main person of the Trinity involved in thought life transformation. He is ready, willing, and able to help you become more than a conqueror (Rom. 8:35–37) in your thought life battles. You can pray specifically to him, asking him to warn you when a careless thought is leading you down the wrong path.

He will certainly answer this prayer, so you had better be ready to hear what he has to say. You may become more uncomfortable with certain people, conversations, television shows, and so on. Remember, he wants the best for you, and anything he "pings" you about is for your greater good.

The Holy Spirit will enlighten you to the truth (John 16:33). By meditating on God's Word, you declare that God is the ruler of your mind. His truth will defeat the lies you encounter in the fight against yourself, your enemy, and others. God's Word will help you tear down Satan's strongholds one day at a time.

The Holy Spirit teaches us and reminds us of Jesus's words. The more you study God's Word and meditate on it, the more the Holy Spirit will bring God's truth to your mind at the perfect time. I'm always amazed at the Holy Spirit's ability to bring an ideally suited Scripture to mind right when I need it, after I've done the work of hiding it inside.

The Holy Spirit is also interceding for you (Rom. 8:27). He is praying on your behalf, asking God the Father to renew your mind. You're not alone on this renewal journey; you have a member of the Triune God working all the time for your benefit!

Take hope knowing that the Holy Spirit is your Mediator, Advocate, and Counselor. He will equip you and defend you before Satan. He will guide you into fruitful thinking rather than careless thinking. He also counsels you to grow your faith and understanding.

�֍ THE DISCIPLINE OF MEDITATION

The theme verse for this chapter is an excellent meditation prompt any time your thoughts turn careless. Let's look at 2 Corinthians 10:5 closely.

We take captive every thought

Remember catching fireflies when you were a little girl? Once you captured the firefly in a jar, you could study it up close. You could watch it crawl around, count its legs, and marvel at its blinking light. The firefly wasn't distant anymore—it was under your inspection.

Taking your thoughts captive is like catching fireflies. You need to hold the thoughts closely for a moment, examining them for what they are. Don't make any excuses for them; just study them closely.

to make it obedient to Christ.

When you examine your thoughts, you need to ask yourself, "Is this thought obedient to Christ?" Another way of processing it is to ask yourself, "Would I feel good about sharing this thought aloud with Jesus?" If your thought doesn't pass through this filter, you can quickly confess it and turn in a different direction to get back on the obedience path.

The discipline of meditation is not intended to create a heavy load of guilt. It's simply capturing and filtering thoughts to have a mind more like Jesus. He knows that we can't possibly process every thought that travels through our minds. Yet the more discipline we apply, the more thoughts will go through the obedience filter, and the more obedient we will become.

Write the verse:

_____

_____

_____

_____

_____

Your thoughts:

_____

_____

_____

_____

_____

❁ MORE MEDITATION VERSES

Here are several additional verses to help you transform careless thoughts into obedient thoughts. Use them in your meditation time today.

Test me, LORD, and try me, examine my heart and my mind. (Ps. 26:2)

You will keep in perfect peace those whose minds are steadfast, because they trust in you. (Isa. 26:3)

Do not conform to the pattern of this world, but be transformed by the renewing of your mind. Then you will be able to test and approve what God's will is—his good, pleasing and perfect will. (Rom. 12:2)

Prayer

Heavenly Father,

I praise you because you masterfully created a world of order. You designed my mind to be ordered as well.

I confess that I often allow my thoughts to carelessly stray into places where they don't belong. I admit that sometimes I choose to go to those wayward places, and I want to make changes today.

Thank you for offering me life and peace through a renewed mind. Thank you for giving me the Holy Spirit as my guide, helper, and teacher. You have promised to never leave me or forsake me, and I trust that you won't leave me alone in my thought life transformation.

Help me capture my careless thoughts and see them for what they are without getting defensive. Help me meditate upon your Word so I have it ready to go when temptation strikes.

In Jesus's name,

Amen.

REFLECTION QUESTIONS

1. What is the connection between one of your current problems and your thought life?

2. What is your biggest area of struggle: fighting yourself, fighting the enemy, or fighting others? Why?

3. Which of the Holy Spirit's roles comforts you most in this thought life renewal process?

TWO

NEGATIVE THOUGHTS

The precepts of the Lord are right, giving joy to the
 heart.
The commands of the Lord are radiant, giving life to
 the eyes.

Psalm 19:8

Have you taken a personality test before? I think they are fascinating and fun. I'm an INFJ on the Myers-Briggs scale and a one with a nine wing on the Enneagram.

The common thread between all the tests I've taken is my glass-half-empty perspective. I'm melancholy, which means I'm a highly sensitive person. Lows are a little lower for me than for most people, and it takes more effort for me to choose a positive perspective.

I not only have a negative bent, but I had lots of negative experiences as a child. My parents divorced when I was four, which cast a permanent shadow of negativity over my life. My family also had a negative communication style when we were stressed or hurting. We simply repeated the same sad stories rather than reaching out for professional help. No matter which house I was in, I was affected by generational patterns of negativity.

Negative thoughts dominated my mind as a teenager. I leaked them out into my journals. The only person who knew how negative I felt was my best friend. When she moved away in our junior year of high school, I was devastated. I thought no one in the world understood me, and my thoughts grew darker.

That autumn, my thoughts were so heavy that they felt like a physical weight. Kind of like the vest you wear when you get dental X-rays. Those pessimistic thoughts rained down on me from a gray cloud that wouldn't go away, and soon I was trapped in a deep pit of depression.

But God had a rescue plan for me. One day after school, I was lying in bed and deciding on which destructive plan to take. I picked one in my thoughts. Right then, I suddenly became aware of God's warm, comforting presence in the room. It was so real I could almost feel it.

The Holy Spirit whispered this message to my spirit: "You don't need to think these thoughts anymore." He knew exactly what I had been thinking and pulled me out of that downward spiral. I got up out of bed, shaken but hopeful. I never considered taking my own life again.

Looking back at that moment now, I see that God cared deeply about my thought life. He knew that my negative thoughts were literally leading me on a path toward death, and he wanted me to choose the path of life. That late autumn afternoon was a turning point in my thought life. I knew my thoughts counted for something, and I knew they had to change.

In the years to follow, I still had many negative circumstances and relationships to sort out. But starting at age sixteen, I began choosing positive thoughts even though my natural bent falls toward negative thoughts. I also chose to surround myself with optimistic friends. One of my dear friends always has sunshine to share, and I value her uplifting perspective. But I know she sometimes struggles with pessimism too. Even the sunniest people are prone to negative thoughts.

Whether you have a naturally optimistic or melancholy personality, you engage in a fight with negative thoughts every single day. With the Holy Spirit's help, we can choose joy instead of negativity.

❊ THE POWER OF JOYFUL THOUGHTS

Joy can help us counteract negative thoughts. It's not the same as happiness, which depends on our circumstances. Happiness is content as long as the sun is shining. But joy can find reasons to celebrate even on a cold, windy, rainy day.

To be joyful, we must learn to be content. In 2 Corinthians 6, the apostle Paul lists many hardships he and his team endured. Within his painful list, he speaks of joy in verse 10. The source of Paul's joy is the same for us: worshipping and serving the one true God.

When we have joy, we don't pretend that our problems have disappeared. Joy helps us find peace in the middle of pain because God is good no matter what. Joy looks forward to a brighter future when no suffering, tears, or negativity will exist (Rev. 21:4).

We can focus on joy when we hope in the treasures God has waiting for us. When you have a heavenly mindset rather than an earthly mindset, joyful thoughts are easier to find. The first chapter of Ephesians is a treasure chest full of God's blessings that we can enjoy both now and in the future. Let's meditate on some of these blessings from the New Living Translation. Read over them slowly, savoring the riches:

All praise to God, the Father of our Lord Jesus Christ, who has blessed us with every spiritual blessing in the heavenly realms because we are united with Christ. (Eph. 1:3)

When we believe, we are united with Christ. That's when we receive every spiritual blessing, like joy, peace, and hope.

Even before he made the world, God loved us and chose us in Christ to be holy and without fault in his eyes. (Eph. 1:4)

God chose you to be his daughter long before you were born. Because Jesus died for you, he sees you as flawless and beautiful.

God decided in advance to adopt us into his own family by bringing us to himself through Jesus Christ. This is what he wanted to do, and it gave him great pleasure. (Eph. 1:5)

Your Father God took great pleasure in adopting you into his heavenly family. He chose you because he loves you so much!

He has showered his kindness on us, along with all wisdom and understanding. (Eph. 1:8)

God showers blessing after blessing on you. He looks upon you with kindness, grants you spiritual understanding, and gives you his perfect wisdom.

And when you believed in Christ, he identified you as his own by giving you the Holy Spirit, whom he promised long ago. (Eph. 1:13b)

One of the best gifts God has given you is the constant presence of the Holy Spirit. This is a fulfillment of a promise he made long before you existed.

The Spirit is God's guarantee that he will give us the inheritance he promised and that he has purchased us to be his own people. He did this so we would praise and glorify him. (Eph. 1:14)

The Holy Spirit's presence in your life guarantees that you will receive heavenly blessings someday. For all this and more, you can praise and glorify his name!

When you are struggling with negative thoughts, you can open this treasure chest up to meditate on your identity in Christ. Joy will rise in your heart when you remember the Bible truths, which can help you overcome negative thoughts.

❀ Meditate on God's Word

Our world is full of pain, and it will drag us down if we allow it. Author Tracie Miles writes, "Any negative thought that goes uncaptured will eventually cause us to sink."[1] Joy can be a life preserver that helps rescue us from a sea of negative thoughts.

Job was a man of much suffering. He lost all his children and his wealth in one day, then lost his health. And he was innocent—he did nothing to deserve his horrible losses. Yet in all his pain, Job attributed his source of joy to God's Word. Look at Job 6:10. I think it's safe to say that Job still holds the Olympic record for suffering. Very few people have suffered as many losses in as short of a time span. If Job could choose joy in God's Word despite his situation, we can too.

Let's look at the theme verse for this chapter to learn more about the source of joy:

> *The precepts of the Lord are right,*
> *giving joy to the heart.*

When you need joy in your heart, you may not first think to look at the precepts (rules) in God's Word. But because God is a loving Father who wants the best for you, you can find joy in meditating on that fact. He will protect you, guide you, and lead you on a path filled with the best things in life that money can't buy.

> *The commands of the Lord are radiant,*
> *giving life to the eyes.*

Wouldn't you love to have your life path lit up before you, so you can walk ahead with clear vision and joy? The teachings and commands in God's Word are like a road map for the Christian life. They give life to our eyes with their radiant truth.

Write the verse:

_____

_____

_____

_____

_____

Your thoughts:

_____

_____

_____

_____

_____

�֍ JOY-BOOSTING THOUGHT EXERCISES

No other book in the Bible lists joy more often than Psalms. Meditating on the Psalms will give you many ways to replace negative thoughts with joyful ones.

God encourages us to put on a joyful, glad, and happy attitude in Psalm 68:3. It's easy to be negative with all the troubles we face each day. But joy is the way we show Jesus to the world, and it's important that we choose to put it on.

Psalm 90:14 tells us that we can find joy by seeking God's love in the morning. Rather than starting off your day with a grumpy attitude, you can praise one aspect of God's character. This will help reset your attitude throughout the day, and you'll feel better. Other people will notice too.

We can find joy in nature while we meditate on Psalm 65:8. Every day, praise God for something you find in nature, whether it's a bird song, flower, sunset, or starry night. When negative thoughts pester you, focus your gaze on God's creation, and you'll find reasons to rejoice.

Psalm 16:11 tells us that the path of life leads to joy. When you are seeking the path God wants you to take, God will give you joy and pleasure if you choose to walk beside him.

God urges us to dance with joy in Psalm 30:11. If you love to dance, you can turn your dancing into a praise session before God. Isn't it wonderful that God gives us creative ways to praise him?

Psalm 43:4 shows us that we can choose joy through music. You can use your singing voice to praise God today. Are you a musician? Use your instrument to play a praise song for him.

God prompts us to recount our blessings in Psalm 126:3, which will inspire joy and cancel out negative thoughts. You can start a daily habit of reviewing all the things God has done for you. This will bring you not only joy but peace and thankfulness as well.

Anytime you need fresh inspiration for countering your negative thoughts, simply enter "joy" in the search box on biblegateway.com and go to the book of Psalms. Pick the translation you like best and use God's Word as your source for busting negativity.

Choose one of the psalms above that stood out to you and write it out below for better memory. Then write about how it will help you choose joy.

Write the verse:

_____

_____

_____

_____

_____

Your thoughts:

_____

_____

_____

_____

_____

❈ MORE MEDITATION VERSES

He will yet fill your mouth with laughter and your lips with shouts of joy. (Job 8:21)

But the angel said to them, "Do not be afraid. I bring you good news that will cause great joy for all the people." (Luke 2:10)

Until now you have not asked for anything in my name. Ask and you will receive, and your joy will be complete. (John 16:24)

May the God of hope fill you with all joy and peace as you trust in him, so that you may overflow with hope by the power of the Holy Spirit. (Rom. 15:13)

Though you have not seen him, you love him; and even though you do not see him now, you believe in him and are filled with an inexpressible and glorious joy. (1 Pet. 1:8)

Prayer

Heavenly Father,

I praise you because you love me, chose me, and share such great blessings with me. How wonderful it is that you consider me your princess!

I confess that I often allow negativity to block you as my source of joy. I know that life will be full of challenges and problems, but that doesn't mean I have to stay stuck in negativity. Today, I choose joy.

Thank you for providing abundant verses on joy in your Word. I trust that you will help me learn the truth of your Word to transform my thinking.

Help me select verses of Scripture that will lift me up when negativity threatens to drown me. With the help of your Holy Spirit, I can renew my mind.

In Jesus's name,
Amen.

REFLECTION QUESTIONS

1. How have your past experiences impacted your struggle with negative thoughts?

2. Which verse in Ephesians 1 means the most to you, and why?

3. Do you have a favorite verse from the book of Psalms? How can you use it to transform your negative thoughts?

THREE

ANXIOUS THOUGHTS

Search me, O God, and know my heart; test me and
know my anxious thoughts.

Psalm 139:23

I t was my turn to stand at the teacher's podium and give a
speech. In English class, we had to turn to a classmate, con-
duct a get-to-know-you interview, and deliver it to the class
in a creative way. I chose to tell the story from the viewpoint of my
classmate's dog.

Hoping for a few grins or chuckles for my creativity, all I was
met with was blank stares from my classmates. I did what you
aren't supposed to do: fixed my eyes on my notes to stop looking
up at my peers, whom I perceived to be disapproving. At the end
of the speech, I slunk into my desk seat, hiding my red face behind
the curtains of my long hair.

No one else took such a weird approach. They shared funny
stories from childhood since they had known each other for so
long. They laughed at each other's shares, while mine had fallen
flat. I wished I could disappear in between the cracks of the school
floor tiles.

At the beginning of freshman year, I had transferred from a
small private school class of twenty-four that felt like family to
a large class of almost three hundred strangers in public school. A
nonathletic introvert, I hadn't had many opportunities to get to
know public school kids beforehand, which made the transition

more difficult. The big crowds felt threatening, especially when I endured being bullied later that year. I never got over feeling like an outsider.

My mild social anxiety persisted through my high school years. I checked out early from school dances and pretty much avoided all the special senior year activities. Though I still live in the same town, I haven't attended any of my high school reunions. Decades later, I still feel like I'm standing on the outside of the in-the-know group.

When I'm not at my best, that same social anxiety flares up if I bump into one of those people here locally. I spot them and my anxiety starts in my stomach, then pushes up my esophagus and makes it harder for me to breathe. My heart races, and I force myself to take deep breaths to calm down. Often, I'll steer my cart into a different store aisle just to avoid a meeting.

My maiden surname means "to take flight" in German. I'm no pro at flying; boarding an airplane produces an altogether different type of anxiety in me. Yet I'm a pro at taking flight from social pressure because the anxiety that seizes my gut pushes me up and away.

✾ YOUR KIND OF ANXIETY

Maybe social anxiety is your struggle, or maybe it isn't. But I'm almost certain you struggle with some form of anxiety. In fact, 70 percent of teens say that anxiety and depression are major problems for them and their peers, and only 4 percent say those aren't problems at all.[1]

Perhaps you are anxious about getting good grades, like six out of ten girls are.[2] I understand that pressure as a high achiever myself. Anything less than an A-minus wasn't acceptable to me. Perfectionism went hand-in-hand with my anxiety as a student.

Thirty-six percent of girls feel nervous about their day.[3] You may worry about looking your best, fitting in with the crowd, or doing well in your extracurricular activities. You might be anxious about relationships with boys or family members. I'm writing this book during the quarantine for the coronavirus pandemic, a virus that has introduced a whole host of new anxieties for the entire world. If you're looking for a new reason to have anxiety, it's not hard to find one at all.

However, God does not want us to be consumed with anxiety during all our waking moments. He designed us to live in his perfect peace, no matter which anxieties we face, large or small. You can choose peace instead of anxiety through Christian meditation. It will truly renew your mind in this area, which Satan desperately desires to conquer.

This chapter is not meant to address anxiety disorders that require medication to control. It's meant to address the roots of anxiety common to most of us, who allow anxiety to take over our minds without even realizing it. But when you know what triggers your anxiety, you can overcome it with the truth of God's Word.

Let's meditate on our chapter theme verse, Psalm 139:23, to discover your triggers so that you can deal with them starting today.

Search me, O God, and know my heart

Do you realize that God knows everything that goes on in your heart and mind? He's already got tabs on your personal triggers that activate anxiety, and he wants to help you identify those thoughts so you can make progress because he loves you so much.

test me and know my anxious thoughts.

When you ask God to search you, know you, and test you, he will most certainly answer that prayer. The Holy Spirit will begin to show you exactly which anxious thoughts you have and where they reside. He'll start pointing them out when they zip through your mind, trying to speed by without being noticed. Like a good cop, he will help you catch them, arrest them, and remove their power over you.

Write the verse:

_____
_____
_____
_____
_____

Your thoughts:

_____
_____
_____
_____
_____

❀ WHEN ANXIETY THREATENS

Consider the physical sensations you have when you are anxious. I know I'm anxious when my insides tighten, my breath shortens, and my heart starts racing. Sometimes it feels like I'm being strangled when anxiety takes hold.

The original meaning of the word *worry* is "to strangle or choke." Author Linda Dillow says, "The stranglehold of worry keeps a woman from enjoying a life of contentment and peace."[4] What happens to your body when worry takes over? Knowing this can help you identify anxiety and deal with it right away.

One day, my husband lost his wallet. All morning, I prayed off and on that he would find it. I ordered lunch from a drive-through. As I sat in line, I noticed my insides tightening. I was imagining the worst—a criminal maxing out our credit cards. Satan was using that moment to set up a foothold of worry, which increased with every heartbeat.

Then the Holy Spirit spoke to me: *What verse can you meditate on right now?* I took a moment to capture my thoughts, then remembered the verse displayed on a card in my kitchen windowsill: "Call upon me in the day of trouble: I will deliver you, and you shall glorify me" (Ps. 50:15 ESV).

I repeated this verse out loud, again and again, then turned it into a prayer. I remembered many other people in the Bible who faced greater problems than mine and how God delivered them. I promised to glorify God and give him all the credit if the wallet was found. Calm washed over me as I prayed.

Later that day, my husband told me his wallet had fallen out of his pocket. It landed on his own jobsite. The wallet was never in a stranger's hands. It was always in God's care. I gave God praise for growing my faith with that little test and thanked him for the verse that kept me on the right track.

Dealing with Anxiety through Meditation

The Bible offers a rich variety of verses to help us deal with anxiety. Let's look at several together, which you can use as shields and arrows in your battles.

Proverbs 12:25 tells us that anxiety weighs our hearts down. Does anxiety or worry feel heavy to you? When anxiety weighs me down, an encouraging word from a friend or loved one lifts me up. But if I'm alone, I can still be uplifted with a positive Scripture about God's character. If you want your heart to feel lighter, you must offload anxious thoughts.

Most of us have not just one but a multitude of anxieties. I love Psalm 94:19 (NKJV) because it tells me that God offers comfort to offset the weight of anxieties. The Latin root for *comfort* is the same one we use for *fortress*, a symbol of strength. God's comfort is intended to strengthen us in our battles. Since you aren't facing your battle in your own power, his supernatural strength can bring you delight.

The short, sweet verse of 1 Peter 5:7 reminds us that God is strong enough to handle all your anxieties. Though they are surely too heavy for you, they aren't too heavy for him. This verse tells us that God handles our anxieties because he loves us so much.

❋ PURSUING PEACE

To truly conquer anxiety, we must focus our thoughts on peace. As a young woman, anxiety ruled my life. God used the book *Calm My Anxious Heart* to set me free from the paralyzing grip of anxiety.

In the book, Linda Dillow refers to God as the Blessed Controller of all things, as found in 1 Timothy 6:15 (Phillips).[5] Her book helped me see that my anxiety struggle was rooted in my desire to have control. Yet that control belongs only to God, who is sovereign over every detail of my life. He showed me that when I put 1 Peter 5:7 into action in my mind, he allowed his peace to enter the places where anxiety once took up space. Since his perfect peace is firmly fixed in my heart, I don't battle anxiety every day like I once did.

The type of peace Jesus gives us is miraculous. This peace carries us through the most difficult circumstances. In John 14:27, Jesus promises to give us peace that is different from the temporary peace the world offers, which depends on circumstances. His perfect peace will drive fear from our hearts and still our troubles into calm trust.

Jesus spoke these words to his disciples on the night before he died. He knew the disciples would be filled with anxiety as they watched him suffer and die and then worried that they may be captured and killed as well. Right before all that happened, Jesus offered peace to his disciples. He told them not to let their hearts be troubled because he knew Satan would tempt them to be consumed with worry. He offered them perfect peace to carry them through the worst anxiety they had ever faced.

Jesus offers the same peace to you. The Bible tells us to "seek peace and pursue it" in Psalm 34:14. When anxiety rises, you must actively search for peace. God provides the peace, but you must pursue it. You can fix verses in your mind so that you're ready when the battle ensues.

Philippians 4:6–7 offers a four-part action plan to help you pursue peace.

1. Pray about everything that causes anxiety. Every anxiety-producing trigger is a charge to ask the Blessed Controller for help.

2. Tell God exactly what you need. Be specific, whether the request is large or small. Anxiety's power drains away when you list your requests to God.

3. Thank him for all he has done. Remember God's faithfulness to you in other times of anxiety. This will help you have faith that he'll pull you through again.

4. Rest in the peace that fills your heart. After you release your anxiety through requests and thanksgiving, God's peace will set a guard over your heart and mind. His peace will set you free to live in obedience, even if your anxious circumstance hasn't changed.

This Scripture is so practical that it's worth memorizing. Write it on a card you can carry with you or put it in the notes section of your phone. Put it into action when anxiety threatens, and your peace will be restored.

Write the verses:

_____

_____

_____

_____

_____

Your thoughts:

_____

_____

_____

_____

_____

❀ MORE MEDITATION VERSES

A heart at peace gives life to the body. (Prov. 14:30)

You will keep in perfect peace those whose minds are steadfast, because they trust in you. (Isa. 26:3)

Lord, you establish peace for us; all that we have accomplished you have done for us. (Isa. 26:12)

The fruit of that righteousness will be peace; its effect will be quietness and confidence forever. (Isa. 32:17)

You will go out in joy and be led forth in peace. (Isa. 55:12)

Therefore, since we have been made right in God's sight by faith, we have peace with God because of what Jesus Christ our Lord has done for us. (Rom. 5:1 NLT)

Stand firm then . . . with your feet fitted with the readiness that comes from the gospel of peace. (Eph. 6:14–15)

Let the peace of Christ rule in your hearts, since as members of one body you were called to peace. (Col. 3:15)

Now may the Lord of peace himself give you peace at all times and in every way. The Lord be with all of you. (2 Thess. 3:16)

Prayer

Heavenly Father,

I praise you as the Blessed Controller over every detail of my life. You know my heart and my mind better than anyone else, and they belong to you for your glory.

I confess that I am often anxious. I admit that my anxiety is often connected to a desire to control my circumstances. Today I declare that only you have control over my life.

Thank you for being faithful to me in the past. Thank you for never leaving me alone in my worries. You have delivered me time and time again, and I trust that you will help me replace anxiety with your perfect peace.

Send your Holy Spirit to reveal my anxiety triggers. Show me the multitude of my anxieties and help me conquer each one through the power of your Word.

In Jesus's name,

Amen.

REFLECTION QUESTIONS

1. What are the physical symptoms of anxiety for you?

2. When do you feel most anxious? Times of day, month, and year? These are the best times to meditate on God's Word.

3. Which verse gave you the most peace? How can you use it to fight off anxiety?

FOUR

SELF-CRITICAL THOUGHTS

I praise you because I am fearfully and wonderfully
made;
your works are wonderful, I know that full well.

Psalm 139:14

Before I turned nine years old, my body started changing into that of a young woman. That's when my DNA started sending messages to my lower stomach to form what I named my hump. My DNA was programmed with directions from one side of my family, where the hump had formed on women's bodies for generations. Yet my hump was so strange to me that I couldn't resist attacking it with self-criticism. I tried to negate it with vicious words in my head.

My hump has made me look two or three months pregnant ever since. I quickly learned that hiding my hump was a major priority because other children didn't hide their criticism of it. No matter how thin I got, my hump has always been part of me. The more I weigh, the bigger it is, but it shrinks if I lose weight. It's a sort of indicator for when I need to eat less and exercise more.

Many times, I've thought I wouldn't look or feel so odd if my hump were gone. Of course, that's also when I study myself in the mirror and find other things I'd like to change. My mind moves downward in a self-critical spiral.

A few years ago, I was drying off after my shower and caught a full-length glimpse of myself in the mirror. Before turning away in my normal disgust, God whisper-shouted to me, *"You are fearfully and wonderfully made—LOOK!"* He led me to look at myself—my whole body—and call it good. Even my hump. When I called my hump "good" for the first time, I felt a new peace come over me. I opened my heart to loving my body just the way it is, without wishing for change.

The hard truth is that God knew ahead of time that I would have a hump because he programmed my DNA cells. This wasn't easy for me to accept because it doesn't make much sense to me. But the more I learned about God, the more I realized I cannot call anything he made "bad." He knew what he was doing, and even though I don't understand it, he understands me perfectly as my Master Designer.

I'm sure that you have a particular body part, inherited trait, or quirky characteristic that you cannot stand. You probably don't know what God was thinking when he gave it to you. Maybe you don't like the way you sound when you talk or laugh. Maybe you simply don't like yourself, period.

I am well acquainted with that self-destructive internal dialogue many of us experience but none of us freely discuss. You aren't alone in this battle. God wants to transform your self-criticism with his love.

❊ TESTING FOR SELF-CRITICISM

How often do words like these go through your mind unchecked?

- stupid
- worthless
- bad
- dumb
- ignorant

- ugly
- annoying
- weird
- fat
- idiot
- loser
- lazy
- too much
- not enough

We may *never* say these words to describe others, at least out loud, but many of us apply these labels to ourselves *every day.* I challenge you to tally these internal criticisms in a notebook for a week. You will be shocked at how many times you are tearing yourself down with self-critical thoughts.

Do you hear those words in an accusing voice? Those words are always tagged with "you are" in my mind. *You are so stupid. You're too fat. You are not enough.* "You are" can be fighting words if followed by a negative. That's exactly what Satan does. The accuser engages us in a fight against ourselves to distract us from God's purposes.

If Satan can keep us busy with daily self-criticism, his battle is half won. He knows that if we don't see ourselves the way God sees us, we cannot fully love others the way God desires. Our family members, friends, classmates, teachers, coaches, and even strangers indirectly suffer from our lack of self-love. But we suffer most of all from self-criticism because we live a life that's a shadow of the one God longs to live with us.

Susie Larson writes, "Do you know what nourishes the soul? It's knowing (and believing) that we are the object of God's intimate and powerful love."[1] What we need is a healthy view of God's love toward us, so we can love ourselves the way he calls us to do, which will then flow over onto others. We can meditate on God's Word to reprogram our self-criticism into reminders of his love, which will heal and transform us.

❄ THE MANY FORMS OF GOD'S LOVE

As you read through these scriptures about God's love, apply them directly to yourself. Place your name inside the verse when it fits. Think of these verses as God's personally penned love letters to you. By contemplating the many ways God loves you, you can silence those critical remarks from your inner judge.

GOD LOVES YOU

Never forget that God's love for you is costly and precious. In 1 John 4:9–10, God shows how he gave up his Son for you, so you could spend eternity in heaven with him. These verses wrap us in God's loving arms, demonstrating that God loved you before you could return your love to him.

Jesus told his disciples to remain in his love because he loved them just as the Father loved him (John 15:9). Ponder this deep thought: the Holy Father loves the sinless Son with perfect love. Jesus loves us with this exact kind of love, every moment of every day. You can return to this astounding love whenever you like through Christian meditation.

Any young woman who honestly declares she loves God is secure in his love. He promises to reveal himself to you if you seek to know him with your whole heart and mind. You must pursue him actively, as described in Proverbs 8:17.

Because of our sinful natures, we don't deserve to be God's daughters. Like the prodigal son in Luke 15, we tentatively return to him, thinking we'd be content only to be his slaves. But our heavenly Father welcomes us with an intimate embrace, kissing us and holding us close. He calls you his child in 1 John 3:1. If you ever doubt your worth, you can find affirmation by meditating on this verse.

God Delights in You

When you delight in someone, you greatly enjoy their company. That's why God always watches over you, caring for you tenderly. He doesn't simply tolerate you; he chose you to be his own. He delights in you and keeps you safe (Ps. 18:19).

God directs every detail of your life. Isn't that amazing? Think of all the mundane day-to-day moments you experience, even the ones that pass *your* notice because they are so familiar. The Bible says that even the hairs on your head are numbered (Matt. 10:30). God knows all your details and treasures them because you matter so much to him, as described in Psalm 37:23.

God Saves You

Whatever battle you are facing, God is waiting for you to call on him for help, so he can save you. He is glorified when you praise him for saving you. He wants to save you from your enemies, just like he saved David from his many enemies, including King Saul (Ps. 18:3).

God patiently listens to all your prayers. When you cry for help, he is glad to save you and draw you closer to him. He welcomes your desperate cries. He is ready to be your Savior who helps you in all your troubles (Ps. 34:6).

God Rescues You

Think about all the troubles you've faced in the past week, month, or year. How has God rescued you from each one? How has he grown your faith through each trial? Do you see the ways God has rescued you every time (Ps. 34:19)? Meditation can help you recall those times of rescue so you can trust God more.

If you're on God's team, he rescues you and keeps you safe. Nothing can come between you and God's love for you (see Rom. 8:38–39). Unlike your inner judge, God does not condemn you. He protects you as a valuable servant (Ps. 34:22).

GOD PROTECTS YOU

Isn't it comforting to know that you have a hiding place when you draw close to God? He is protecting you from many troubles you cannot even see in the spiritual realm. He is surrounding you with songs of victory in the heavenly places (Ps. 32:7).

Psalm 91:4 paints a beautiful word picture of God's gentle loving-kindness. Like a mother duck brings her little ducklings under her wings in a storm, God softly covers you with faithfulness when hard times come. The next time you feel insecure, picture yourself under his loving, protective wings.

GOD UPHOLDS YOU

I love the idea of God holding me up with his strong, holy hand when I feel low. I can't lift myself out of my struggles, but God will uphold me. Isaiah 41:10 helps me rise above my troubles in God's strength and righteousness.

When you feel desperate and cling to God in hope, your Father is holding you up in front of Satan, showing him that he cannot snatch you out of God's hand. Psalm 63:8 says that God holds you up with his right hand. In ancient times, fathers blessed their children with their right hands. God's right hand blesses you as his beloved child.

Are you still struggling to accept the fact that God loves you? That you are a treasure and a delight to him? If so, make it your goal in the next few weeks to meditate on verses that demonstrate God's love for you.

Remember the phrase "If you don't have anything good to say, then don't say anything at all"? Tracie Miles says, "While this is often said in reference to what we say about others, it can also be applied to what we say about ourselves."[2] In those times when you aren't feeling so great about yourself, simply don't say anything bad at all. Refocus your thoughts instead on praising God for how much he loves you.

✻ THINK DIFFERENTLY ABOUT YOURSELF

In my opinion, Psalm 139 is the ultimate affirmation of God's love and care for us. Maybe you know that God called all of his creation good at the beginning but never thought about how this truth applies to you. Psalm 139 is a great tool to use when you're trying to determine your worth while looking in the mirror. Let's meditate on our theme verse for this chapter.

I praise you because I am fearfully and wonderfully made

You are fearfully and wonderfully made. If you've ever seen an artistic masterpiece in a museum, you may have used these words to describe it. You are God's masterpiece! Even if you aren't as far along as you'd like to be, you're the pinnacle of God's creation.

your works are wonderful, I know that full well.

Chrystal Evans Hurst writes, "You are allowed to be both a masterpiece and a work in progress simultaneously."[3] Think about this quote in relation to the verse. You were a masterpiece as a baby and as a little girl. You are a masterpiece now as well. You are still a work in progress, but God is continually renewing you as his treasured masterpiece.

Can you now sincerely agree that you are fearfully and wonderfully made? I encourage you to say this verse out loud right now, declaring to your inner judge and to Satan that you believe the truth about yourself, starting today.

Write the verse:

_____
_____
_____
_____
_____

Your thoughts:

_____
_____
_____
_____
_____

❋ APPLYING GOD'S LOVE TO YOUR THOUGHTS

Make a vow today to stop tearing yourself down. You can speak God's truth to your inner judge and to Satan each time a self-critical thought enters your mind.

When it comes to your body image, remember that the enemy will continually attack you in this area. Alli Worthington writes, "The enemy is a master of distracting and hurting women of God by keeping us busy hating how we look."[4] Don't let the enemy gain ground over you in this area. Commit this area to prayer, asking God to help you see your body the way he sees it, as described in Psalm 139.

If you need to get healthier, don't let your current struggle take over your thought life. You may need to make some changes so you can be the best version of the young woman God called you to be. But it doesn't mean your thought life has to suffer in the process. Meditate on verses that inspire you and invite God into your journey toward better health. One of my favorites is 1 Timothy 4:8.

For physical training is of some value

When you train your body, you will be in the best shape for serving God. For this reason, make exercise, rest, nutrition, and self-care high priorities.

but godliness has value for all things

God cares about your physical health, but he cares even more about your spiritual health. Pursuing godliness blesses every part of your life and blesses others in the process.

*holding promise for both the present
life and the life to come.*

The efforts you put into your spiritual health matter both now and in heaven. Everything you do to glorify God with your body is important to him.

Write the verse:

_____

_____

_____

_____

_____

Your thoughts:

_____

_____

_____

_____

_____

Don't let the mirror condemn you anymore. Instead, post sticky notes of Bible verses on it to inspire meditation. You can use the mirror to give God glory.

❀ MORE MEDITATION VERSES

Here are a few verses from Psalm 139 for inspiration. Choose your favorite Bible version and meditate on the whole psalm.

O Lord, you have examined my heart and know everything about me. (Ps. 139:1 NLT)

You go before me and follow me.
You place your hand of blessing on my head. (Ps. 139:5 NLT)

You made all the delicate, inner parts of my body
and knit me together in my mother's womb.
    (Ps. 139:13 NLT)

Prayer

Heavenly Father,

I praise you for making me your masterpiece, God. I am amazed at your love for me.

I confess that I often criticize myself in my mind, which is against your will for me. Today I want to start replacing those thoughts with the truth about how much you love me, which will help me love myself.

Thank you for showing me new ways to think. I want to change so I can love you better, treat myself right, and let your love in me overflow to others.

Give me a keen awareness of the times when I'm being self-critical. Help me change from the inside out with conviction from the Holy Spirit. Renew my mind with your healing power.

In Jesus's name,

Amen.

REFLECTION QUESTIONS

1. What is your least favorite body part? How has this chapter helped you see it as good?

2. What words can you pull from the scriptures to fight back against accusing thoughts? Ideas: I am God's delight; I am loved by God; God rescues me.

3. How will you redeem your time in front of the mirror?

FIVE

THOUGHTS THAT CRITICIZE OTHERS

Why do you look at the speck of sawdust in your
brother's eye and pay no attention to the plank in
your own eye?

Matthew 7:3

Though I have been bullied several times in my life, I was a
bully myself for a season. Back in middle school, I pestered
and mocked a classmate for months, to the point that she
considered changing schools. That's when the cover blew off my
sabotage, and the ugly mess spilled out for everyone to see.

At the time, I couldn't have linked this to the bullying, but I
was dealing with major stress at home. My tendency was to turn
my anger inward. But this time, my stress-fueled anger was toxic
enough to spill over onto someone else. An innocent classmate
became the perfect target because no one expected good-girl me
to be so mean.

Everyone at school called me Miss Perfect until this nasty secret
unfolded. When confronted, I felt relief at not needing to keep up
the game any longer. I sincerely apologized and repented. The girl
and I even became good friends through high school. However,
I've never forgotten my dark side that is tempted to lash out in
criticism of others.

In Chapter Two, I mentioned that I'm an INFJ on the Myers-
Briggs personality test. The J stands for judging. Most of the time,
this means I use God-given discernment to determine what is right

and what is wrong. The dark side of this strength is my constant temptation to criticize others. It's my main character flaw. Only through God's grace and by meditating on his Word have I been able to get a handle on it.

We live in a flaw-picking world. We watch shows where food, clothing, and personal style are critiqued. Most of us look at the critical reviews before we watch a video or consider a purchase. On social media, people feel free to spout off criticism in ways they'd never do in person. Though none of us like to *receive* criticism, we often feel justified in dishing it out.

When was the last time you were criticized in an unloving way? I can remember word-for-word what my offenders have said, whether in person or online. Their critical words sink deep, and we'll address offenses like that in Chapter Twelve. The value you can gain from considering your own hurt feelings after criticism can help you think twice before criticizing someone else.

If we know how badly criticism hurts, why do we do it? In my mind, it's because I secretly desire to feel better than other people. Those thoughts are based on insecurity because when I feel secure in who I am, I don't feel like putting others down just to make myself feel better. I feel icky admitting that to you. But I'm guessing you've dealt with this before as well.

The bottom line is that God is the only perfect judge. I have no right to judge someone else because I can't see into his or her heart the way God can. Only God is able to deliver perfect justice. When I'm tempted to criticize others, I'm learning to surrender my inner critic's seat to God, who is the only one worthy to sit on a judgment throne.

Let's look at the differences between harmful criticism and constructive criticism.

❋ HARMFUL CRITICISM

Harmful criticism starts when we unfairly label others. Whether their actions are truly wrong or simply not our preference, we first cast judgment in our minds. If we let the thoughts fester, judgment seeps out in our words and actions. We must address those harmfully critical thoughts before we speak, write, or act them out.

You always have the opportunity to speak the truth in love, which is the opposite of harmful criticism. But this requires a thoughtful, self-controlled approach, which can be cultivated through meditation. Let's meditate on the ways God warns us against criticizing others in Matthew 7:3.

*Why do you look at the speck of
sawdust in your brother's eye*

To see a speck of sawdust in someone's eye, you need to get really close. Unless they're inviting you to help them remove the irritation, you are invading their personal space without permission. That's the definition of being rude, and in 1 Corinthians 13, we learn that love is not rude. Love is kind.

and pay no attention to the plank in your own eye?

Jesus is telling us that we must deal with our own long list of sins before even thinking about criticizing others. Only then will we be humble enough to help someone else, and that's also only after they grant us permission in a time-tested relationship.

Write the verse:

_____

_____

_____

_____

Your thoughts:

_____

_____

_____

_____

_____

In John 8:7, Jesus was speaking to a crowd of Pharisees, ready to stone a woman who had been caught in adultery. One by one, the men dropped their stones and walked away after Jesus's convicting statement. I can't throw a stone at someone when I'm dealing with the same issue. I also can't sling a stone even if I'm *not* dealing with that issue, since I have my own plank-sized problems to keep me occupied.

The apostle James warns us against criticizing one another in James 4:11–12. He says that when we judge others, we are also judging God's laws. God is holy, and therefore the only qualified lawgiver and judge in the universe. We have no right to take his place—we are far from qualified. Focusing on God's holy role as judge helps us see that we are equals with other people in God's eyes.

Jesus was direct when he told us to stop judging others so that we will not be judged (Luke 6:37). His words are simple to read but not so easy to follow. We can meditate on this verse and turn it into a prayer, asking God to help us refrain from holding onto judgment, condemnation, and unforgiveness. The phrases are short enough to memorize, so you can call them to mind every time you are tempted to judge.

❁ CONSTRUCTIVE CRITICISM

As a college art major, I had weekly critiques in my illustration class. We would pin our works to the wall and take turns offering tips for improvement. One day my teacher pointed out that my classmate's design would look better if he toned down the yellow-green in his design to not clash with the reds. But he couldn't see it.

The rest of us noticed it too, especially when the teacher went up to the board and pointed out the area of concern. He insisted that he'd used a blue-green there. But when the teacher asked him to show her the colored pencil he'd used, the problem became clear. He said, "I'm color-blind." His eyes were not seeing things like the rest of ours. He needed that critique to improve his design.

We need constructive criticism like this because we can't see our own blind spots. When others offer this type of criticism, it's for our good. We can offer constructive criticism to bless and encourage others. By controlling your mind before offering criticism, you can be a blessing. You can increase your wisdom on when to offer this type of criticism through meditation.

You don't have the right to speak truth into someone's life unless they know you care about them. Otherwise, it's pure judgment that will cause destruction. Cultivating a relationship before you confront someone is essential.

Rather than tearing someone down in your mind, consider ways to build them up (1 Thess. 5:11). Think of reasons to praise rather than reasons to criticize. God will transform your thoughts so you can be an encourager instead of a critic. You can learn how to act like Jesus by meditating on Ephesians 4:15.

Instead, speaking the truth in love

Speaking the truth in love takes a lot of practice and prayer. You'll need to grant yourself grace, and ask others for grace, when you get this wrong. As you work on speaking the truth in love, keep meditating on God's Word to stay on track.

we will in all things grow up into him

You will experience spiritual growth as you practice speaking the truth in love. Jesus always spoke the truth, and he always spoke it in love. You become more like him every time you use constructive criticism rather than harmful criticism.

who is the Head, that is, Christ.

In this chapter of Ephesians, Paul is writing about the body of Christ. As believers, we are all members of this body, and Jesus Christ is the head. In order to speak the words of Jesus to others, we must strive to speak the truth in love. Look to Jesus as your example.

Write the verse:

_____
_____
_____
_____
_____

Your thoughts:

_____
_____
_____
_____
_____

✿ PURSUING KINDNESS

Kindness is a sweet, healing balm that has great potential to reverse the trend of criticism in our culture. When you think kind thoughts, they turn into kind words. They help transform you so that you respond like Christ rather than respond like the world. Kindness helps you serve as salt and light in your circles of influence.

In her book *The Kindness Challenge*, Shaunti Feldhahn challenges you to not speak a negative word against someone for thirty days. To do this, you must change your thoughts first. Kindness gives you the power to change even your most difficult relationships.

Are you surprised that kindness has this ability? Feldhahn writes, "True kindness always strengthens and empowers, never weakens. It changes you, not just others. It melts hardness and makes gentleness immensely powerful."[1] But she admits that kindness is delicate enough to be destroyed unless we practice it with intention.

I took this challenge toward a truly difficult person in my life. Even though our relationship didn't improve after those thirty days, my attitude toward her softened. I began to think compassionate thoughts toward her because I saw how her contentious ways drove many people away. I started praying for her even though she shunned my kindness. When I didn't need to interact with her anymore, I parted with peace in my heart rather than bitterness. Kindness changed my attitude in a tough situation, and I'm grateful it proved more powerful than criticism.

Kindness replaces our criticism with a healthy sense of control. We can't change others, but we can control our thoughts and responses toward them. In this way, we benefit ourselves and benefit others. Criticism, by contrast, is cruel and brings destruction (Prov. 11:17).

Since we are chosen and loved by God, he wants to clothe us in his beautiful robes. They are woven with threads of kindness, which are interwoven with compassion, humility, gentleness, and patience. All these lovely virtues involve blessing others rather than protecting our self-interests. Meditate on Colossians 3:12, asking God to help you "wear" each of these virtues.

Critical thoughts stir up contention. When we let these thoughts escape our minds, quarrels may break out. God calls us to a different kind of living. He wants us to show kindness without resentment, so we can freely teach others how to grow in faith. You can meditate on 2 Timothy 2:24 to become more like Jesus.

Kindness helps us make connections with people we may have criticized before. God may surprise us if we lay criticism aside and give kindness a try. Jesus showed kindness to outsiders—prostitutes, cheaters, drunkards, and lepers. But the Son of God spoke his harshest words of criticism against religious people who set themselves up as judges. Meditating on verses about kindness, compassion, and loving others has melted away the hard edges of the *J* in my personality, which stands more for *Jesus* than for *Judge* now. Let's meditate on a sweet verse about kindness, Proverbs 16:24.

Kind words are like honey

Who doesn't like sweet things? Our tongues have receptors for sweet foods because we are created by God to crave sweetness. All of us have a craving to receive kindness too. Since you crave kindness from others, go first to show it to them and pray that it is returned.

sweet to the soul and healthy for the body.

Honey has restorative qualities that can benefit our immune systems. It also contains trace minerals that are good for our bodies. Kindness is healing for our soul and blesses our bodies with floods of good-feeling hormones, which boost our immune systems. Kindness really does work wonders in many ways. Go ahead—share it today to boost someone's physical and spiritual health.

Write the verse:

_____

_____

_____

_____

_____

Your thoughts:

_____

_____

_____

_____

_____

✿ MORE MEDITATION VERSES

Your love for one another will prove to the world that you are my disciples. (John 13:35 NLT)

This is my commandment: Love each other in the same way I have loved you. (John 15:12 NLT)

Above all, love each other deeply, because love covers over a multitude of sins. (1 Pet. 4:8)

Whoever claims to love God yet hates a brother or sister is a liar. (1 John 4:20a)

Prayer

Heavenly Father,

I praise you because you show me kindness. You don't criticize me, but you lovingly correct me when necessary. You are the perfect teacher for showing me how to treat others.

I confess that I think critical thoughts toward others and sometimes carry them over into words and actions. I'm sorry for the times I hurt others with criticism. Clean my heart and mind from toxic habits of flaw-picking, suspicion, and cruelty toward others.

Thank you for giving me hope that I can change. Thank you, Jesus, for providing many examples of how you always spoke the truth in love.

Teach me how to replace criticism with kindness. Start the transformation in my heart and mind, and then carry it over into my actions, words, and body language. Show me how to make new connections with those I may have criticized before.

In Jesus's name,
Amen.

REFLECTION QUESTIONS

1. In what ways are you tempted to criticize others most?

2. What are the roots of your criticism of others? Did you see it modeled as you grew up? Did others criticize you? Pray that God will remove that root from your heart so you can heal.

3. Which verses will you use to instantly fight off critical thoughts of others?

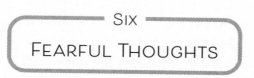

Six

FEARFUL THOUGHTS

There is no fear in love, but perfect love casts out fear.

1 John 4:18a ESV

The fear of abandonment has haunted me all my life as a child of divorce. Even though I was only four years old at the time, I vividly remember the day my father left. I knew something was wrong when I saw him crying for the first time. Then I saw the suitcase in his hand. A claw of terror gripped my throat and silenced me as he hugged me goodbye.

When he drove away, my deepest fear took hold and never let go. It has colored every relationship I've ever had with a male. In the back of my mind, I'm always thinking, *He's going to leave you someday.*

As a young woman, I was still haunted by this fear. One day I drove to the banks of the Tennessee River with my Bible, asking God to give me a verse for comfort. By those peaceful waters, I opened my Bible to Hebrews 13:5 (NKJV), which reads, "I will never leave you nor forsake you." The powerful verse didn't completely heal me that day, but God planted it in my thoughts to slowly take root.

Now as a married woman, panicked thoughts still run through my mind at vulnerable moments, especially when my husband hasn't called to say he'll be late. But every time those fears haunt me, I declare that verse aloud: "God will never leave me nor forsake me."

Even if a worst-case scenario does play out, God will still be with me, and I've learned to trust him by meditating on Hebrews 13:5.

I wish that the fear of abandonment were the only one to haunt me. For example, I fear carnival rides, and it's not from a lack of trying to ride them. My fear of heights is so bad that I can't get three steps up a ladder without breaking into a full-body sweat. Spiders send me into a panic, and sometimes I feel fearful in large crowds.

What are your fears? I know you have a few haunting you. I'm guessing your oldest fears have to do with deep hurts, like my fear of abandonment. If your parents are married, you may fear they will get divorced. Maybe you have fears over your health or your future. Perhaps rejection is your top fear. No matter what fear haunts you, God will help you overcome it with courage, which you can grow through Christian meditation.

❋ FACING OUR DEEPEST FEARS

Whatever your deepest fear is, God wants to help you face it. He doesn't want it haunting you for years. He wants to quiet your fear with his loving presence. Our theme verse, 1 John 4:18a (ESV), will help you face your deepest fear and draw close in relationship to God.

There is no fear in love

In Chapter Four, we talked about God's love as an antidote. When we are secure in his love, our fears are quieted because God himself is love.

but perfect love casts out fear.

Since my deepest fear is attached to a father wound, I have specifically worked on developing trust in my perfect heavenly Father. When I am afraid, I imagine climbing into his lap and letting him hold me. In that safe place, I meditate on the truths in his Word, and my fears subside. There, I find perfect peace and love, which heals all my fear-ridden places.

I know many of you reading this also have father wounds. I know how hard it is to trust your heavenly Father when your earthly father destroyed your trust. But if you choose verses that speak about God's kindness and faithfulness as your Father and meditate on them regularly, the Holy Spirit will begin to rebuild your trust.

Write the verse:

_____

_____

_____

_____

_____

Your thoughts:

_____

_____

_____

_____

_____

If you suffer from the fear of abandonment like me, Psalm 27:10 may feel like it was personally written for you. It says that even if your parents abandon you, God holds you close. By regularly meditating on this psalm, you can let God heal your fear.

Though earthly fathers sometimes forsake their children, God steps in as Father to all who are abandoned. He is high and holy, yet he is close to you because you are precious to him. He defines himself as your Father and Defender in Psalm 68:5.

You may feel like a slave to your fears. Perhaps you feel as if your fears control you, and you may never break free of them. This is not how your heavenly Father wants you to feel. He is a loving Father who brings you into his own family, and he loves hearing you call him Daddy (Rom. 8:15 NLT).

Meditating on verses about God as your Father can help you face your fears with greater courage. Knowing that God is bigger than your fear can give you peace in the scariest times. Believing that God controls the terms of your deepest fear can help you relax in his loving arms. Trusting that God has a plan and purpose for you despite your fear can help you find hope.

❀ Conquering Our Fears

When I was young, my sister and a family friend begged me to play with them in the field behind the house. But first, we had to climb over the gate. My fear of heights prevented me from climbing. When I tried to swing my leg over the top of the gate, I started trembling. Embarrassed, I would step down, head back inside, and read my books, feeling trapped by fear.

Our fears limit us. They hold us captive. They steal possibilities away from us. In our own strength, we can't overcome our worst fears. But with God's help, we can conquer them.

Psalm 18 is one of my favorite Bible passages. Verse 29 tells us that we can scale a wall and crush an army with God's strength (NLT). When I think of scaling a wall, I think about the ease a lizard has scurrying up my garage wall. With no fear at all, the little lizard climbs to crazy heights.

Even though I'm too afraid to climb over a gate, much less scale a wall, God has helped me over many emotional walls that I once thought impossible to conquer. In his strength alone we can cast our fears aside and shimmy up whatever wall we're facing.

Maria Furlough writes, "Our fears are not trustworthy. They are not based on truth, they do not know facts, and they are guilty of vast exaggeration. Our fears do not love us, they do not care for us, they take no account of our pain or our sorrow. Our fears are unworthy of our attention. They do not deserve the deepest parts of us, nor do they deserve our attention or our allegiance."[1]

When your fears are closing in on you, you can turn to Isaiah 35:4 (NLT) for help. It says that God will destroy your enemies and save you. God will destroy the power Satan wages against you. He will save you from spiritual attacks. You don't need to give in to fear because God is fighting your battles for you.

Did you know that God promises to hold your hand when you are afraid? (See Isa. 41:13.) When I was a depressed teen, my mom encouraged me to ask Jesus to hold my hand at the beginning of the school day and remember he was holding it throughout the day. Even though I felt a little silly doing it, I pretended Jesus was walking around holding my hand, and I gained comfort knowing he was near me in my trials. In times when you face trials and fear threatens, you can ask Jesus to hold your hand too.

Pursuing Courage

Jesus sometimes asks us to step out of our comfort zones and join him in a journey that requires us to pass through fear with courage. Late one night his disciples were in a boat on the Sea of Galilee. Jesus came walking to them on the water, and they were understandably shaken. But Jesus told them, "Take courage! It is I. Don't be afraid" (Matt. 14:27).

When Peter said he wanted to walk out on the water, Jesus called him. Peter walked on water for a few moments but lost courage when he saw the wind and waves. When he began to sink, Jesus reached out his hand and rescued Peter, pulling him safely back into the boat.

How long would Peter have walked on the water if he had kept his focus on Jesus? We don't know. Yet Jesus would have allowed Peter to experience more of his power if he hadn't given into his fear.

Is Jesus calling you out of your fear to do something new that feels scary? Do you hear him telling you to take courage and keep your eyes fixed on him? If so, your fear may not subside until you obey. You may need to walk right through it to get where Jesus is calling you.

Jennie Allen writes, "Jesus isn't scolding us for being afraid; He is calling us out of our comfortable boats to do something unthinkable, something that is only possible with His power."[2] What is he calling you to do that requires you to take courage?

When I need courage, I turn to one of the most familiar psalms in the Bible: Psalm 23. I meditate on verse four and gain peace, strength, and courage from it.

> *Even though I walk through the valley*
> *of the shadow of death*

When you walk through a valley, the darkness feels deeper if the shadow of death looms over it. You may have walked through valleys of sickness, brokenness, or dashed dreams. These valleys are where Satan loves to tempt us to feel scared and unsafe.

> *I will fear no evil, for you are with me*

Because God is right beside us in each of our valleys, we can choose courage instead of fear. You can count on Satan having his evil arrows pointed at you in the valley. But Jesus's strong, loving presence will guide us safely through.

> *your rod and your staff, they comfort me.*

Psalm 23 is the picture of Jesus as the Good Shepherd. A shepherd uses his staff and rod to protect sheep from predators. When you are fighting fear while walking through valleys, remember that the rod and staff of God's Word are protecting you. By meditating on it in the dark valleys, you can get through with comfort and courage.

Write the verse:

_____

_____

_____

_____

_____

Your thoughts:

_____

_____

_____

_____

_____

After the Israelites had wandered the desert for forty years, it was time for Joshua to move God's people into the Promised Land. God knew the bridge between the desert and the Promised Land was called Courage. He told Joshua over and over to "be strong and very courageous." God also said, "Be careful to obey all the law my servant Moses gave you; do not turn from it to the right or to the left, that you may be successful wherever you go" (Josh. 1:7). God will show us the right path to take as we step forward in courage.

Sometimes courage also requires waiting, as noted in Psalm 27:14. When you're afraid, waiting is the last thing you want to do. You simply want the fearful situation to be over with. But God can use the waiting period to build your faith. Your courage can grow as you wait for God to relieve you from your fears.

We can have courage even during suffering because Jesus has already won the ultimate victory for us (John 16:33). When I faced fearful trials that had unknown endings, I had to look my fear of abandonment in the eye and realize that Jesus had already won the battle for me. He didn't take my suffering away, but he gave me peace in the middle of it and built my courage in the process.

You can step out in faith by meditating on God's Word as you face your fears. Jesus may even ask you to walk on water with him so he gets more glory and you gain more courage.

❋ MORE MEDITATION VERSES

The Lord is my light and my salvation—whom shall I fear? The Lord is the strength of my life—of whom shall I be afraid? (Ps. 27:1)

God is our refuge and strength, always ready to help in times of trouble. So we will not fear when earthquakes come and the mountains crumble into the sea. (Ps. 46:1–2 NLT)

When I am afraid, I put my trust in you. (Ps. 56:3)

For God has not given us a spirit of fear and timidity, but of power, love and self-discipline. (2 Tim. 1:7 NLT)

Prayer

Heavenly Father,

I praise you because you are perfect love, and there is no fear in your presence. I am glad I can always feel safe with you. I confess that, too often, I let fear take control over my life. I let fear limit my choices and steal my opportunities. My fear keeps me from living the life of faith you want me to live.

Thank you for granting me courage to overcome my fears. Thank you, Jesus, for winning the ultimate victory for me. I don't have to face my fears alone, and I thank you for always walking beside me.

Help me choose courage when I feel afraid. Inspire me to trust you more every day so that my faith is stronger and my courage grows.

In Jesus's name,

Amen.

REFLECTION QUESTIONS

1. What is your deepest, oldest fear?

2. How do you typically handle your fears? How will you change your method to deepen your trust in God?

3. What verses will you memorize to fight off fears when they arise?

SEVEN

IDOLATROUS THOUGHTS

Their land is full of idols; they bow down to the work of
their hands, to what their fingers have made.

Isaiah 2:8

On Valentine's Day during my freshman year of college, I stopped by my car between morning classes. To my great delight, I found a pink rose under my windshield wiper. Since it was freezing outside, I waited to get inside my car before finding out who sent me the flower.

Boy-crazy was a label that had fit me for a long time. Though I was far from a flirt, I had a collection of secret crushes dating back to kindergarten. There was nothing—*nothing*—I wanted more than a boyfriend. My yearning for the perfect guy was a constant ache.

With cartoon hearts clouding my vision, I eagerly opened the valentine. The rose was from . . . my mom. I sighed with disappointment, then guilt. Her words were kind and loving. I did appreciate them. But my unwanted yearning appeared again. When would I get a rose from a boy who liked me as much as I liked him?

I didn't know it at the time, but I was worshipping an idol called Boyfriend. This idol looked handsome, strong, charming, and secure. With him, I thought I'd never feel sad, lonely, or scared again. I admired him and displayed him proudly on a little throne in my heart. He was my goal to pursue. My dream to be fulfilled. Without him, I felt frightened and empty.

A few years later, I thought getting married would take away my longing. Surely a husband was even better than a boyfriend! But when I replaced the Boyfriend idol with the Husband idol, the ache didn't go away. I was shocked with disappointment.

It took me a long time to learn that when I set anything except God on the throne of my heart, I still feel unfulfilled. Even good things like relationships can become idols if we see them as our source of security and fulfillment. When you feel like you can't live without something, that's a sign you have an idol in your life.

❈ CONTEMPORARY IDOL WORSHIP

Idol worship today is sophisticated. Satan uses sneaky tactics to dress idols up as innocent or reasonable so as not to reveal their devastating potential. Like the beautiful fruit on the tree of the knowledge of good and evil, our idols have the appearance of helping and sustaining us rather than presenting harm.

Maybe your idol is small and shiny, like a smartphone you simply can't put down. After all, your generation is the first to grow up with smartphones, and you probably can't remember life before the internet.[1] The majority of your peers are connected to smartphones every waking hour of every day.

You can have more than one idol, of course. You may idolize a celebrity, a beautiful wardrobe, career path, romantic relationship, or any number of other good things that sit on your heart's throne instead of God. As you read this chapter, ask God to reveal the idols you may not even recognize.

Jennifer Dukes Lee writes, "At the root of idolatry is the cunning twisting of truth. Cool gifts from God—like sex, food, and even happiness—become nooses slipped around our spiritual necks. The enemy convinces us that anything God made is better in excess."[2] Look for areas of excess in your life, and you'll soon find your idol.

Scripture is clear that idol worship brings suffering to our hearts and strife into our relationship with God. God takes idol worship seriously and considers it deadly for our spiritual health. When we meditate on verses about idolatry, we can see the idols for what they really are and can tear them down, one by one.

When we prioritize something or someone over God, we stir his jealousy (Deut. 32:16). Though our jealousy is sinful, God's jealousy is holy. When we choose an idol over him, he burns with heartache and righteous anger. Think about how you would feel if your boyfriend or best friend dumped you for someone else. That's how God feels when you prioritize an idol.

God longs for a face-to-face relationship with you. Idols strip away that relationship. God doesn't turn his back on you, but you turn your back on him when you choose an idol (see 1 Kings 14:9b). Choices that may seem unimportant or excusable to you offend God. This truth may be hard to hear, but it shows how much God loves you.

Our idols can become snares that bind us (Ps. 106:36). Walking into a spiderweb can be a shock. It's chaotic and stressful to quickly remove near-invisible threads while wondering if a spider is about to bite you. Idol worship also snares us, one step at a time. Before we know it, we will be in slavery to an idol that is wrapped all around our hearts. It can unexpectedly bite us before we realize how far we are from God.

God sometimes uses blunt words to wake us up to the truth about idol worship. Idols are worthless and cause us to become worthless (Jer. 2:5b). When we worship idols, we are worthless in service to others, powerless to bless others, and hopeless in relationship to God. The more power we give our idols, the more isolated and cut off from the body of believers we become. That's Satan's main goal—to keep us far away from God and others. If an idol can help him accomplish that goal, he'll make it as enticing as possible. Let's look closely at Jonah 2:8 to tell ourselves the truth.

Those who cling to worthless idols

When you were young, did you have a lovie you couldn't live without? Children cling to these items when they are separating from their moms but still need a feeling of security. You are too grown-up for such things now. But if you are clinging to an idol, it's like you're dragging a smelly, old, worthless thing around instead of choosing to cling to Jesus, your worthy Savior and Friend.

turn away from God's love for them.

God's heart is broken when we worship idols. God freely offers us his love. Yet we reject his love when we cling to idols as our primary source of comfort. Notice the love thread running through this verse and all the verses above. Consider God's great love for you when he prompts you to destroy the idols in your heart. He's there waiting to replace them with his boundless love.

Write the verse:

_____
_____
_____
_____
_____

Your thoughts:

_____
_____
_____
_____
_____

❀ RENOUNCING IDOLS

Getting rid of idols is a tough task. Satan will engage in hand-to-hand combat as you tear them down. But the Bible promises blessings to you as you begin the process.

The first step in letting go of idols is admitting that they cannot provide for you. Place your hope in God when you are tempted to turn to your idol for comfort, and he will show you the riches of all he provides. Your idols are empty and vain, but you can trust God to meet your needs (Jer. 14:22).

Try going a week without your idol and see how you feel. The stronger the hold it has on you, the more you will be tempted to turn back to it. When you are tempted to beat yourself up for turning back to it, meditate on Ezekiel 36:25–27.

> *I will sprinkle clean water on you, and you*
> *will be clean; I will cleanse you from all your*
> *impurities and from all your idols.*

When we worship idols, we are unclean in God's eyes. But he promises to cleanse us from idol worship. We can't do that work on our own because our hearts will always lean toward idol worship. Draw comfort from the fact that God is with you in this struggle.

> *I will give you a new heart and put a new spirit in you*

When we commit to worshipping God alone, he gives us a new heart and new spirit. He delights in your smallest efforts to turn back to him, and he'll meet you where you are. This verse can give you hope for a fresh start.

> *I will remove from you your heart of stone*
> *and give you a heart of flesh.*

The longer you worship an idol, the harder your heart becomes toward God. But when your heart is soft, it is sensitive to God. Ask God to turn your stony ways into softness as you work to become idol-free.

> *And I will put my Spirit in you and move you to follow my decrees and be careful to keep my laws.*

The Holy Spirit will help you fight off the temptation to return to your idols. When you meditate on God's Word, he will remind you of God's requirements. You will become more like Jesus with every step you take away from your idols.

Write the verses:

_____
_____
_____
_____
_____

Your thoughts:

_____
_____
_____
_____
_____

You may be tempted to be casual about removing idols. But you must be deliberate. Break, smash, cut, or burn your idol down; make a permanent change (Deut. 7:5). Do whatever is needed to completely remove the idol's power from your life. God will grant you discernment. For example, you may need to limit your screen time or end a toxic relationship. If he leads you to give something up for good, you won't regret trusting and obeying him.

✽ DEVOTING YOUR HEART TO GOD

Trusting an unseen God with your whole heart isn't easy. But I've learned it is the only life worth living. As he stripped away my Boyfriend idol, I learned that God's presence is the only one that can fulfill all my needs. An idol can never do that.

Elisabeth Elliot writes, "If we hold tightly to anything given to us, unwilling to let it go when the time comes to let it go or unwilling to allow it to be used as the Giver means it to be used, we stunt the growth of the soul."[3] My soul wasn't growing when I attached my heart's desires to an idol. But it did grow when I fully devoted my heart to God.

Devotion requires faithfulness and a daily cultivation of relationship with God through meditation, study, prayer, and worship. I promise that the more devoted you are to following God, the less idols will appeal to you.

Ezra was a scribe and servant who enjoyed a close relationship with God, since he devoted himself to studying and observing God's law (Ezra 7:1–10). You can also live a life devoted to God by studying and observing God's law. The most devoted followers of God I've known have all made a commitment to regular study of his Word. You can enjoy closeness with God when you make the same commitment.

Another key to living the devoted life is worshipping God with other believers. The members of the early church were devoted to fellowship, listening to the apostles' teachings, prayer, and sharing meals together (Acts 2:42). Your local church will help you stay devoted in your walk with God.

A natural outflow of our devotion to God is love for other people. Your local church provides opportunities to serve others in love. God never intended you to be alone. He wants you to demonstrate your devotion to him by serving others. Romans 12:10 is the perfect meditation verse to spur you to action.

The Bible tells us to be devoted in prayer (Col. 4:2). Prayer is an ongoing conversation with God that you can have from the moment you wake up until the time you close your eyes for sleep. As you develop a habit of prayer, your heart's devotion to God will grow deep roots, and you'll enjoy the blessings of a close relationship with him.

Devotion to God will help you make better choices (Titus 2:12). Since I've gotten serious about my faith, my idols aren't as enticing as they used to be. As you destroy your idols and choose to be devoted to God, he will renew your mind to be more like that of Jesus, who lived a life of total devotion to his Father's will. Matthew 10:39 shows us the devotion Jesus wants us to have.

If you cling to your life, you will lose it

Nothing we own, desire, or need should come before God. As Christians, we must fully surrender not only our idols but also our whole lives over for God's glory. Clinging to your idols will leave you with empty hands in the end.

but if you give up your life for me, you will find it.

This verse is a great paradox, but it's the only way to free ourselves from the slavery of idol worship. To find the abundant life God promises for us, we must fully devote our hearts to him. Devotion to God is the ultimate cure for idol worship.

❀ MORE MEDITATION VERSES

Do not turn away after useless idols. They can do you no good, nor can they rescue you, because they are useless. (1 Sam. 12:21)

Protect me, for I am devoted to you. Save me, for I serve you and trust you. You are my God. (Ps. 86:2 NLT)

I am the LORD; that is my name! I will not give my glory to anyone else. I will not share my praise with carved idols. (Isa. 42:8 NLT)

Prayer

Heavenly Father,

I praise you because no one is higher than you. You are my source of security, comfort, provision, and hope. You deserve all glory and praise.

I confess that I have allowed idols to take your rightful place in my heart. I am sorry that I choose to put anything above you, for everything I have belongs to you. Help me worship you as the Creator of all things rather than worshipping what you have created.

Thank you for cleansing and purifying me of my sins. I am grateful that you don't turn your back on me forever, Lord. You welcome me when I come to you with a devoted heart.

Show me all the idols standing in the way of a deeper relationship with you. Help me remove them, Lord. I want to devote my heart to you rather than anything else, even the good gifts you give me. I trust you will bless me both now and in heaven for seating you on the throne of my heart.

In Jesus's name,
Amen.

REFLECTION QUESTIONS

1. After reading this chapter, which idol is new to you?

2. Why is it hard for you to put God instead of your idol on the throne of your heart?

3. What can you do differently this week to show devotion to God?

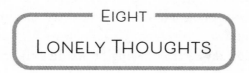

EIGHT
LONELY THOUGHTS

Turn to me and be gracious to me, for I am lonely and afflicted.

Psalm 25:16

In elementary school, most of my classmates greatly anticipated summer break. They couldn't wait to spend lazy days at the pool or travel to the beach. My best friend always took a family vacation out west to see America's great monuments. I listened to their plans as if they were speaking in a foreign language. All of it was unfamiliar to me. I dreaded summers ever since I was ten years old, when my sister and I had to stay home alone while my mom worked.

The daily chores and inevitable boredom were frustrating—no child likes those parts of summer break. But the loneliness was what I dreaded most. Never did I feel more alone than on a summer afternoon. By 3:00 P.M., my sister and I had completed our household tasks, watched our allotted two hours of television, played a few rounds of Parcheesi or Battleship, and read our library books. In the afternoon, the day's energy fell away, and each passing minute slowly ground away my resolve. It seemed like forever until Mom would return home and I'd finally receive a portion of the attention I craved.

On the loneliest afternoons, I'd go to Mom's bedroom and try on her clothes, shoes, and jewelry. This wasn't to imagine what it would feel like to be grown up, like many girls do. I placed those dresses, sweaters, necklaces, and high heels on my body to try to feel her presence. I remembered the times before the divorce when she was a stay-at-home mom and I was relaxed enough to be carefree. Loneliness was the silent, constant presence in my heart and mind that stole my carefree feelings. It was like an invisible jacket I couldn't take off.

I could see, hear, touch, and smell family and friends. I couldn't do any of that with God. In my mind, I knew he was with me, loving me and watching over me. But those truths weren't enough to satisfy my heart. What I craved more than anything else were face-to-face relationships. During the school year, relationships were easier to come by. But in the summer, the void was exposed, and loneliness clung to me.

Loneliness was my constant companion through junior high, high school, college, and beyond. Often, I would settle for toxic friendships or dating relationships in my attempt to shrug lonely feelings off. It took me many years to realize that no one person could satisfy my craving for fellowship. God had to relieve my loneliness with his own warm, loving presence. Once I began seeking him first, I was able to tear off the loneliness jacket, piece by piece.

I still can't see, hear, touch, or smell God. But that's no longer an impossible barrier for me. Since I've spent years drawing closer to him by studying and meditating on his Word, he is more real to me now than my "real" life. Every day, I can't wait to "hear" his voice and interact with him in prayer. However, I had to lay aside everything else in my heart, including my family, to receive healing for loneliness.

❋ DEALING WITH LONELY THOUGHTS

Loneliness is rampant in our isolated culture. Gen Z is currently the loneliest generation of all, according to a large study. Many of you feel that no one knows you very well, that you are shy around others, and that the people around you aren't really with you.[1] A "vast, unsoothable sense of loneliness"[2] is a frequent companion for many of us with divorced parents. But there is hope for us as we learn to draw close to God and others. Meditation can start us on that journey.

Before you turn to anyone else, turn to God to soothe your loneliness. He is the only one who is available for you twenty-four hours a day, seven days a week. Since he made you, he knows you better than anyone else. But he's not only all-present and all-knowing. He longs for you to draw close to him in your loneliest times. When I'm feeling very lonely, I meditate on Song of Solomon 8:3. I picture Jesus embracing me with his left hand under my head and his right arm around me. Lying in this unique prayer position, I often experience the most peaceful moments of my week.

You also need to know the difference between being alone and feeling lonely. Alone is not necessarily an uncomfortable place to be. Every young woman needs to enjoy her own company. You can also enjoy unbroken fellowship with God in those spaces of aloneness. The Bible tells us that Jesus often withdrew to "lonely places" to pray (Luke 5:16). He knew that those times alone with his Father would be free from pressure and distraction. They were perfect places for him to recharge before going back out into the world to fulfill his calling. In your busy life, if you intentionally choose to be alone with Jesus often, you'll be filled up with his presence and better prepared to fulfill your purpose.

In contrast to healthy times of aloneness, lonely times feel painful. They are also open targets for Satan's attacks. During Jesus's temptation, Satan waited until Jesus was at his loneliest point to tempt him (Matt. 4:1–3). He knows that in our loneliest moments, we are most willing to settle for what he has to offer. We're willing to believe his lies to receive relief from our pain. In those moments, you can fight back with Scripture, just like Jesus did. A good verse is the theme verse for this chapter, Psalm 25:16. Let's look at it more closely.

Turn to me and be gracious to me

We can always invite God into our lonely moments. Even though he is high and mighty on his heavenly throne, he loves responding to our cries for his companionship. His turning toward us is an act of grace that we don't deserve, yet we can treasure it as our most valuable possession.

for I am lonely and afflicted.

It's always best to admit the truth before God. By admitting that you are lonely and afflicted (which means to be damaged, harassed, or tormented[3]), you are being vulnerable with the one who loves you most of all. You can memorize this verse and turn it into a prayer when you are facing temptation in your loneliest moments. God will answer it with his loving presence.

Write the verse:

_____
_____
_____
_____
_____

Your thoughts:

_____
_____
_____
_____
_____

❀ PURSUING FELLOWSHIP

It's helpful to look at what God has to say about loneliness. In the Garden of Eden, before sin entered the world and everything was good, God looked at Adam and said it was "not good" for him to be alone (Gen. 2:18). Think about this. In a perfect creation, God called Adam's state of aloneness not good. Why? Because people are made in God's image, and the one true God is three persons in relationship to one another—Father, Son, and Holy Spirit. To be totally alone isn't fully reflecting God's image.

God wants us to be in fellowship with him first. But he also mandates that we be in fellowship with one another. Humans are social creatures, and we need each other to feel fully alive. That's one of the most important lessons I learned in the global pandemic of 2020. We need each other—not just on FaceTime, Zoom calls, or social media. As a wise friend once told me, we all need to be "Jesus with skin on" to each other.

God gives us three gifts: families (Ps. 68:6), friends (John 15:13), and the church (Acts 2:42–47). These people are intended to be the ones who encourage, strengthen, support, and sharpen us (Prov. 27:17). If you have a broken family, friends in the body of Christ can be your father, mother, brother, and sister figures (Mark 3:31–34). You will find healing from loneliness when you seek fellowship from real, live, imperfect people.

But how do you do this? Many girls want friends but don't know how to get them. The Bible has much to say about what to do and what not to do when you want to find friends. Let's use Christian meditation to renew our minds as we think about friendship.

A good friend is faithful no matter what. Jonathan was a trustworthy friend to David, even though he was King Saul's son and David was a shepherd boy. He made a lifelong promise to David because he loved David as he loved himself (1 Sam. 18:3–4). Jonathan went so far as to put his own life in danger as he defended

David to his father (1 Sam. 20:32–33). His friendship with David is a shining example of courage, risk, and commitment.

Friends should not betray or insult one another. David describes how much a friend's betrayal hurt him in Psalm 55:12–14. Gossip is a sure way to destroy a friendship, as noted in Proverbs 16:28. True friends aren't afraid to speak hard truths to each other if it's for the greater good (Prov. 27:6). They give advice that is pleasant to hear (Prov. 27:9). They love one another unconditionally, knowing that God loved them first (1 John 4:11).

When you are lonely, Satan will always tempt you to believe the lie that you're better off alone. But the world needs your contributions as a friend. You can be the kind of friend God describes in the Bible if you reach out in faith. Keep asking, seeking, and knocking for godly friends, and God will open doors for you (Matt. 7:7–8). He will help you ignore Satan's lies as you courageously reach out for new friends. Remember, in a lonely generation yearning for friendship, girls who are willing to reach out first may end up with the best friends of all!

This encouraging passage from Romans 12:4–5 affirms your value as a part of the body of Christ, which is the church. Let's break it down through meditation.

For just as each of us has one body with many members

Our bodies have many different parts that work together as a whole. Each of us needs all our parts if we are to function at our maximum capacity. Though Satan may whisper the lie that you aren't needed in your circles, God affirms that you are much needed in his diverse and beautiful plan.

and these members do not all have the same function

Your eyes can't do the same things as your hands. But who is to say which one is more important? All parts of your body, both seen and unseen, are valuable. People in the church have different functions too. You may have believed Satan's lie that people around you aren't really with you or don't get you. That's because he wants you to hide your gifts from them and keep their gifts hidden from you. As you reach out in friendship, you can discover the beauty of your own gifts, plus the multicolored beauty of others.

so in Christ we, though many, form one body

All the Christians in the world make up the body of Christ. We have different nationalities, races, preferences, and styles of worship. But we all have something unique to offer. This is why it's so important for you to get involved in your local church. When you are actively involved in fellowship, you receive a blessing while blessing others. Cut off from fellowship, you're like a hand or a foot without a body.

and each member belongs to all the others.

As a daughter of the King, you belong in a huge family of brothers and sisters in Christ. Don't miss out on the fellowship in that family. Don't believe that your loneliness is a jacket you'll have to wear for life. Reach out for the fellowship God offers you in the family of believers. You belong to them, and they are a precious gift to you.

Write the verse:

_____

_____

_____

_____

_____

Your thoughts:

_____

_____

_____

_____

_____

❁ MORE MEDITATION VERSES

The LORD is a friend to those who fear him. He teaches them his covenant. (Ps. 25:14 NLT)

The Lord is near to all who call on him, to all who call on him in truth. (Ps. 145:18)

A friend loves at all times. (Prov. 17:17a)

The eye cannot say to the hand, "I don't need you!" And the head cannot say to the feet, "I don't need you!" (1 Cor. 12:21)

Draw near to God, and he will draw near to you. (James 4:8a)

But if we walk in the light, as he is in the light, we have fellowship with one another, and the blood of Jesus, his Son, purifies us from all sin. (1 John 1:7)

Prayer

Heavenly Father,

I praise you for offering friendship to me. Though you are the Creator of all things, you desire friendship with your creation. I marvel at your willingness to be close to me.

I confess that I have believed Satan's lies about loneliness. Too often I haven't been the friend I needed to be, and I have felt sorry for myself rather than reaching out for fellowship. But I have new hope from your Word, Jesus. Help me draw near to you and draw near to others.

Thank you for meeting me in my alone times when I can sort things out with you in prayer. Thank you for my family, my friends, and the church. Thank you in advance for all the relationships you have prepared for me in the future.

Help me ask, seek, and knock for fellowship. I invite you to walk with me as I pursue new friends. Help me believe your truth instead of Satan's lies. I know I can overcome loneliness with you by my side.

In Jesus's name,

Amen.

REFLECTION QUESTIONS

1. When do you feel loneliest?

2. How can you be a friend like the Bible describes?

3. Which verse will be most useful to you for overcoming loneliness? Which one is most inspiring for finding new friends?

NINE

SELF-FOCUSED THOUGHTS

Turn my heart toward your statutes and not toward selfish gain.

Psalm 119:36

I love someone who has been clinically diagnosed with narcissistic personality disorder. People with this disorder have typically been so wounded that they work overtime to preserve their "perfect" masks. Though their actions can be extreme, we all struggle with the same undercurrents of self-focused thoughts.

When I'm around this person, I carefully premeasure my words. No matter how personal the story is to me, the person masterfully turns the story back to center on them. Conversation like this is exhausting. That's why I limit the time I spend with this person, even though I will always love them from a distance.

In studying this person's behavior patterns, I am often tempted to point a finger of accusation. But the more I contemplate this person's extreme actions, the more I see similar (yet more normal) threads of selfishness in my own thought life.

For example, I can easily view a simple misunderstanding as a personal attack. In mere moments, I can throw a big pity party if I dwell on a certain thought too long. A holiday can turn into a hospital for my feelings alone, with little regard for others. Even though I'm not a narcissist, I do struggle with self-centered thoughts. This is true of every human in history.

My past hurts tempt me to feel sorry for myself. As a true victim of emotional abuse, I make a daily choice to refuse the victim mentality. In moments of abuse, a victim cannot be blamed for what is happening to her. But once she has healed, she has the power to throw off Satan's attacks and the temptation to think like a victim. The victim mindset infected me for many years, and I have overcome it only with the truth in God's Word. If you struggle with it yourself, you can find freedom in Christian meditation.

In this chapter, we'll focus on the everyday variety of self-focused thoughts—thoughts that protect our own interests when we need to focus on others. The truth of God's Word can protect us against self-focused thoughts, which run so rampant in our contemporary culture.

The Bible tells us that the closer we come to the time when Jesus returns, the more we will see people become "lovers of themselves" (2 Tim. 3:2). We will likely see greater temptations toward self-focused thoughts in days to come. That's why practicing Christian meditation now will guard your heart and mind today and protect you in the future, keeping you close to God and the truth.

THE DEEP ROOTS OF SELF-FOCUSED THOUGHTS

The first few pages of the Bible show us the roots of self-focused thoughts. When Adam was created, he was given both responsibility for the Garden of Eden and freedom to enjoy it. God gave him only one limit: "You must not eat from the tree of the knowledge of good and evil, for when you eat from it you will certainly die" (Gen. 2:16–17).

In the very next verse, God stated that it was not good (inside a perfect creation!) for Adam to be alone. So he created Eve from one of Adam's ribs and gave them both great blessings and peace.

Satan approached Eve in the form of a serpent and questioned God's limit. This planted seeds of doubt in her mind. She added to God's Word in Genesis 3:3, saying that God told them to not even touch it, though touching the forbidden fruit probably wasn't smart anyway. Then Satan directly contradicted God's Word, planting a giant selfishness seed in her mind: "you will be like God" if you eat the fruit.

Eve knew God as the creator and sustainer of all life. His power, majesty, goodness, and beauty were on bountiful display. She saw a full-color, multidimensional picture of his righteous character.

Eve knew God needed nothing. Creation depended on him, not the other way around. Though she had been created to be dependent on God and her husband, she perceived a sheen of beauty on the idea of not needing anything, just like God. The shell on her selfishness seed began to crack open.

She began rationalizing, and the seed sunk into the soil of her thought life. As she gazed at the fruit, thoughts like these ran through her mind. *How bad can this fruit be? It's perfectly ripe and must be divinely sweet. It's better than all the other fruits because it will grant me special wisdom. A little bite won't hurt.*

In that moment, she forgot that God sees everything, even nibbles of selfishness. His truth was far from her mind when the fruit touched her lips and tongue. Eve was the first human to taste the fruit of self-focused thoughts.

Though Adam was right there with Eve, he didn't stop her. She shared the fruit, and he accepted it. But as they looked into each other's eyes, with the sweet taste still in their mouths, they felt searing shame. Division, fear, blame, pain, curses, and suffering soon followed. Because Eve allowed those self-focused thoughts to take root, all of us have suffered ever since.

In his best-selling book *The Purpose Driven Life*, Rick Warren opens with this sentence: "It's not about you."[1] Why? Because our sinful nature tempts us to see the world as revolving around us. We have made the same bad choices Eve did: rationalizing, questioning God's laws, and forgetting that he's always present. Each one of our sins has pride at its root. Our sinful nature will always believe that we know better than God, and we don't want to be dependent on anyone or anything else.

Selfishness, pride, arrogance, and haughtiness are firmly condemned in Scripture. Consider what God has to say about selfishness and use Scripture to confess and repent from self-focus.

Arrogant people are not welcome in God's presence because their refusal to admit wrong angers him (Ps. 5:5). Those who are arrogant can expect to receive rebuke (Ps. 119:21) and punishment (Prov. 16:5). God is storing up anger for those who live only for themselves (Rom. 2:8). If we don't confess our self-focused thoughts, we'll face these tough consequences.

God takes our self-focused thoughts personally. He refuses to share his glory with anyone (Isa. 2:11). The more blessings we have, the greater temptation we'll have to turn away from him in our arrogance (Ezek. 28:5, Hosea 13:6). God knows that a prideful young woman has no room in her thoughts for him (Ps. 10:4). He promises that pride has a humiliating ending (Prov. 16:18) because he will not put up with a proud heart (Ps. 101:5). These painful lessons are in store for us if we persist in a spirit of pride or arrogance.

❋ ERADICATING SELF-FOCUSED THOUGHTS THROUGH MEDITATION

I enjoy gardening, but it requires a constant battle against weeds. If I don't check my garden every day, weeds will quickly choke out the healthy plants.

Since I live in the woods, I have an extrastrong weed in my rock garden: poison ivy. Its roots go very deep. I can't simply pull it up or keep cutting it back. Because its roots are resistant to normal removal methods, I must use strong chemicals to eradicate poison ivy from where it doesn't belong.

Self-focused thoughts are the same way. Since pride is attached to every sin we commit, we must double down on our efforts to eradicate the seeds and roots of self-focused thoughts from our minds. Satan wants them to spread as far as possible, so they will form a poisonous carpet under every thought. Pray for the Holy Spirit to help you recognize and remove the seeds of these thoughts before they take root and to help you pull up old roots that just won't quit producing vines.

Removing self-focused thoughts from our minds is a lot like receiving discipline from parents. No one enjoys being called out for doing things wrong (Heb. 12:11). But as we clear those noxious weeds from our minds, we grant more growing space for peace and righteousness.

True love isn't self-focused. It is kind, gentle, forgiving, and compassionate to others rather than self-protective (1 Cor. 13:5). Pull up the roots on one of the love plants in your mind and study them for a moment. Ask God to show you if any self-seeking motives are attached. If so, ask for his help in removing them.

Strife is like a hailstorm that batters and weakens the good plants in our thought lives. When we eradicate pride, we stop the storms of strife that we've stirred up ourselves. By choosing to eradicate self-focused thoughts from our thought life through Christian meditation, we will gain wisdom that will calm strife that is rooted in arrogance, as explained in Psalm 119:36.

Turn my heart toward your statutes

The more we meditate on God's statutes (teachings that guide us toward godly living), the more he will dig up the old roots of pride. His teachings guard our hearts against the weeds of self-focused thoughts.

and not toward selfish gain.

God's Word is a preventive treatment, a spray that destroys weed seeds before they ever sprout. When you meditate on it, you'll be protected from self-centered thoughts in advance. He will help you turn from a self-focused path toward right living.

Write the verse:

_____

_____

_____

_____

_____

Your thoughts:

_____

_____

_____

_____

_____

�֍ Pursuing Humility

Humility is like fertilizer that helps healthy thoughts grow in our minds. In John 15, Jesus tells us that he is the vine and we are the branches; we are to abide in him to bear much fruit. We cannot abide in him unless we have a humble, dependent spirit. He wants to reverse the curse Eve received in the garden and plant a new garden in us. But it cannot thrive unless we have a humble spirit that admits that, apart from Jesus, we can do nothing (John 15:5).

Humility strengthens our minds with wisdom (Prov. 11:2), which helps us become better caretakers of our thought lives. We will have an increased ability to weed out self-focused thoughts when we take a humble position toward God and others. Humility brings us honor instead of humiliation, which is a consequence of pride (Prov. 29:23).

Even though our culture values pride over humility, God elevates the humble. He opposes the proud but shows grace to humble people (James 4:6). Jesus himself was the humblest person who ever lived, yet he is also the King of Kings. We can follow his example to form a countercultural pathway in our thought lives.

Beth Moore writes, "Humility is the heart of the great paradox: we find our lives when we lose them to something much larger."[2] God gives grace freely to us when we decide to give our selfishness over to him. He will not resist us; he will give us his best when we desire humility more than pride.

In a culture full of self-promotion, the Holy Spirit is actively seeking those with minds who have the attitude expressed in Psalm 131. He loves taking up residence in believers who are humble and value God more than what the world offers. Our materialistic culture constantly appeals to our self-focused nature. We must fight it through meditation on verses like Proverbs 16:19, especially in those moments when we stare at a piece of "fruit" and begin making excuses for why it would be good to eat.

Romans 12:6 is a pH test for the soil in your mind. If you enjoy the company of regular people, the pH level in your mind is balanced, meaning that good relationships can grow there. If your mind is too acidic with disharmony or too alkaline with arrogance, healthy relationships can't develop. Use the fertilizer of humility to correct the soil and watch your relationships flourish, as described in Philippians 2:3.

Do nothing out of selfish ambition or vain conceit.

Everything we think, say, or do should be tinged with humility rather than a self-focused attitude. Paul uses an absolute word, "nothing," to give us no wiggle room. The more we put this verse into practice, the more we will become like Jesus.

Rather, in humility value others above yourselves.

We show our humility best in relationships with others. God is pleased when we honor him and others with a humble spirit. Keep pulling up self-focused thoughts and sprinkling humility in your thought life, and you will be living life according to God's will.

Write the verse:

_____

_____

_____

_____

_____

Your thoughts:

_____

_____

_____

_____

_____

God promises great rewards for those with a humble spirit (Prov. 22:4). We can expect to receive God's best, in both this life and the next, if we pursue humility.

❋ More Meditation Verses

An unfriendly person pursues selfish ends and against all sound judgment starts quarrels. (Prov. 18:1)

Mockers are proud and haughty; they act with boundless arrogance. (Prov. 21:24 NLT)

Fear of the Lord teaches wisdom; humility precedes honor. (Prov. 15:33 NLT)

For where you have envy and selfish ambition, there you find disorder and every evil practice. (James 3:16)

As it is, you boast in your arrogance. All such boasting is evil. (James 4:16 ESV)

All of you, clothe yourselves with humility toward one another, because, "God opposes the proud but shows favor to the humble." (1 Pet. 5:5b)

Prayer

Heavenly Father,

I praise you for stooping in humility to relate to me. Jesus, you didn't have to leave your throne of glory to save me. But you chose to do so with a humble spirit, and I am in awe of your total lack of selfishness.

I confess that selfishness is my daily battle. Pride is at the root of all my sinful thoughts and actions. I consistently choose only what I want and often believe the lie that I don't need you. I want to repent of my selfish attitudes and keep growing in humility.

Jesus, thank you for modeling humility through many examples in your gospel. Your humility is perfect, inspiring, and so different from how I normally act. But I am grateful you provide a path for me to follow.

Help me destroy the roots of self-focus in my thought life, Lord. Help me identify areas I have ignored or have never recognized before. As I meditate on your Word, make me your humble follower. Give me the courage to pursue your holy will in a culture that values pride over humility.

In Jesus's name,

Amen.

REFLECTION QUESTIONS

1. What new concept did you learn about self-focused thoughts from Eve's story? How can you apply it to your thought life?

2. In your area of biggest struggle with self-focused thoughts, what actions can you take to pull up their roots?

3. In which relationship could you reap the biggest harvest from pursuing humility this week?

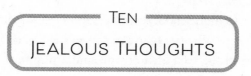

But godliness with contentment is great gain.

1 Timothy 6:6

Every day I love spending time on social media. But it often stirs up something sour in me. It has taught me better than anything else about my hidden tendencies to crave what others have. Their skinny figure I haven't had since prepuberty. Their trendy makeup and clothing I've never been able to pull off with such flair. Their perfectly highlighted hair with no frizz. When visually taking in others' feeds, I so easily forget how much abundance surrounds me in a giant spread.

Since I work from home, social media is my primary way to stay connected with the outside world. I truly treasure the photos, comments, and messages from real-life friends. No one loves a face-to-face meeting more than me—just ask my church friends, who know our regular meetings are one of my weekly highlights. But both in person and online, I've been surprised at how often jealousy has sneaked into my thoughts.

My social media accounts have challenged me to be sincerely happy for those who have what I don't have. It's easy to forget the trade-offs I willingly make. For example, I have a big, beautiful home in the country, but our family takes fewer vacations than our peers. I'm perfectly fine with that fact until I see others' pictures of trips to the beach or the mountains or Paris. Then suddenly the cracks in the ceiling of my home look more obvious to me, and discontentment creeps in.

I was once a high school secretary, and I got to know our office aides pretty well. Whether they came from wealthy or from modest homes, most of the teen girls craved something they didn't have. They wanted a newer car, a nicer prom dress, a fancier phone, or a sweeter singing voice. It seemed like each girl had another girl to whom she compared herself, and whatever the other girl had, she wanted.

Jealousy is a pervasive problem for females of all ages. I'm learning that no matter what life stage I reach and no matter how much abundance I accumulate, jealousy will always be waiting to tempt me.

My friend Deb Wolf wrote an interesting post that has given me a much-needed perspective on being jealous of others. Read this excerpt and reflect on where you stand:

> If the world were one hundred people, thirty would always have enough to eat. Fifty would be malnourished, twenty would be undernourished, and one would be dying of starvation. Forty people live in a country designated as "free," twelve live in a war zone, and sixty can't speak [or] act according to their faith and conscience due to harassment, imprisonment, torture or death. Forty-five people have a computer and forty have an internet connection; seven have a college degree and twelve are unable to read. Ten people have no safe, clean water to drink and thirty-three live without basic sanitation.[1]

I'm guessing you're in nearly all those "luxury" categories if you are reading this book. This list is not meant to make us feel guilty. It's meant to drive us to our knees to thank God for everything we take for granted: shelter, indoor plumbing, clean water, healthy food, electricity, internet connection, education, and freedom.

Please put this book down for a moment and thank God for his abundance to you.

❀ THE ROOT OF JEALOUSY

Our eyes and ears are the doorways for jealousy to enter our thoughts. The ads we see, the social media posts we view, and the commercials we hear all tempt us to crave more. They purposely stir our dissatisfaction so that we will be moved to make a purchase.

I know this from working in advertising for years. There's nothing wrong with the ads themselves; it's how we handle them that matters. They can either feed our jealousy or move us toward gratitude for what we already have.

Comparing our lives with those of others feeds discontentment. Rachel and Leah were two sisters, each jealous of one another. Rachel was the pretty one; Leah was less attractive (Gen. 29:17). Jacob fell in love with Rachel at first sight and promised her father, Laban, he would work for seven years just for the chance to marry her.

When the wedding day arrived, Laban tricked Jacob into marrying Leah instead (Gen. 29:22–23). Can you imagine the heartbreak both sisters felt that night? Rachel didn't get her man, and Leah was a pawn in her father's hands. This marriage was definitely starting off on the wrong foot.

The next morning, Jacob confronted Laban the trickster, who promised to also give Rachel in marriage at the end of the week. But the Bible is honest about the situation that followed: "[Jacob's] love was greater for Rachel than his love for Leah" (Gen. 29:30). It's not that he didn't love Leah, yet he clearly loved Rachel more.

You would think that after all this, Leah would be insanely jealous of Rachel. Her sister was prettier and had captured Jacob's heart with no effort. She must have felt like she couldn't compete. But eventually, the jealousy flowed both ways. Leah was able to have four babies in a row, while Rachel had none. Rachel's jealousy of Leah became so intense that she wanted to die (Gen. 30:1).

However, God had great plans for these sisters. Both women became mothers of the tribes of Israel, God's chosen people. Rachel was the mother of Joseph, who saved his entire family from famine (Gen. 50:20). Leah had an even greater honor. Her son Judah provided the bloodline from which Jesus would be born (Gen. 49:10).

Rachel and Leah were both thrust into a situation they didn't want. They both had inborn characteristics they wished they could change. The Bible never records a reconciliation between the two, but it preserves their story as a sure example of jealousy. Their story is a warning for us because we don't know the plans God has for us either. As with these women, he may choose to use our weaknesses for his glory.

If we intentionally guard our thought lives against comparison, jealousy won't be allowed to enter. We must guard what our eyes see and what our ears hear to block out dissatisfaction with what we have. By making God the Lord over our thought lives, we can cultivate contentment rather than jealousy. He's the only one who can perfectly satisfy the cravings of your heart. When I feel discontent with my possessions, relationships, or other areas, I meditate on Psalm 37:4.

Take delight in the Lord

What delights you? If you delight in what's temporary, jealousy and discontentment will always tempt you. But you can have a full supply of contentment if you delight in God himself.

and he will give you

God promises to give us not only what we need but also what delights us. It's good to be honest with God about what you really want. But delighting in God means delighting in things money can't buy. You can always delight in his unconditional love, peace, goodness, and strength, for example. God is willing to give you everything you want if you delight in the right things.

the desires of your heart.

God challenged me to list all my heart's desires to him. Then he showed me how I can seek ultimate fulfillment of those desires in him. One example is my desire for security, and now he is my most secure place—not my home, bank account, or any relationship. Over time, I've learned the delight in asking him to fill my desires rather than seeking the desires of my heart in the world. You will find greater peace when you do the same.

Write the verse:

_____
_____
_____
_____
_____

Your thoughts:

_____
_____
_____
_____
_____

❁ HANDLING JEALOUSY THROUGH MEDITATION

Jealousy is a human reaction, not a godly response. We can take the higher road by retraining our minds with Christian meditation.

Working hard yet constantly striving for more is the American way. But this pursuit is creating misery. As a culture, we are overweight, stressed out, addicted, and desperate for peace. Our constant striving is meaningless (Eccles. 4:8), but God promises contentment when we delight in him instead of in our wealth.

Not everyone who follows God will be wealthy, at least in the eyes of the world. However, they can prosper and be content in the spiritual places because they are depending on God to meet all their needs, as described in Job 36:11. Obedience and service to God create gratitude and contentment.

The apostle Paul tells us in Philippians 4:11–13 that contentment can be learned. He wrote most of his letters while being imprisoned under conditions that were nothing like those in the orderly prisons of today. He was content while writing with chains around his feet in a dark, dirty Roman cell because he knew God was with him, and his delight was in the Lord.

When Paul was a Pharisee, he enjoyed a much different situation as an upper-class member of society. But after following Jesus, Paul was often homeless, hungry, and without proper clothing. Yet his secret of living with contentment lay in his relationship with Jesus. He trusted Jesus to give him strength in every situation, and we can do the same.

The love of money is often a stumbling block in our pursuit of contentment. Vigilantly guard your heart against the desire to get rich, which is a significant temptation for your generation.[2] Don't think that getting a great job, winning the lottery, or gaining an inheritance will solve all your problems. Every time you are tempted by such thoughts, meditate on 1 Timothy 6:8–10. Remind yourself that you can be content with simple blessings and trust God to provide the rest.

❀ PURSUING THANKSGIVING

God calls us to pursue contentment, and we can arrive at contentment through cultivating thanksgiving every day in Christian meditation.

When I recently saw a Peanuts Happy Journal online, I simply had to have it. Most of my journals hold painful thoughts and memories, but this one is only for the good stuff. My lists include perfectly ripe strawberries, kind words from friends, and times the Holy Spirit sent the ideal book or song to me in masterful timing. When I record those thankful things, jealousy is miles away.

When I find a verse that sparks gratitude, I record it in my happy journal as well. Writing out that verse seals it in my memory and provides a shield against discontentment.

Ann Voskamp writes, "Thanksgiving is necessary to live the well, whole, *fullest* life."[3] When we offer our gratitude and thanksgiving to God, we are choosing a fuller, richer life with more heavenly blessings than earthly blessings. A life of peace and contentment, no matter how much we have or don't have.

Jesus modeled thankfulness for us. In front of the giant crowd about to be miraculously fed, Jesus made sure to give thanks (John 6:11). God calls us to be more like Jesus every day, which includes being thankful for everything we receive. He wants us to be thankful at mealtimes and all other times of the day, whether we have a simple meal or a sumptuous feast.

The Bible tells us to be genuine in our thankfulness. Look up 1 Thessalonians 5:18 and pay attention to the phrase "in all circumstances"—note that it's not "for all circumstances." We can be thankful *in* all circumstances, abundant or sparse, because God wants us to be thankful just as Jesus was thankful. The more we practice thankfulness, the more we will become like our Savior.

Receiving a tough situation with gratitude is a mark of spiritual maturity. You can choose to look for the good in whatever situation

God gives you (1 Tim. 4:4). Fight off discontentment by remembering that everything you receive first passes through God's hands. Thanksgiving is an act of submission that will help you trust God more. You can cultivate contentment and gratitude by meditating on Hebrews 13:5a.

Keep your lives free from the love of money

How do you keep your life free from the love of money? Guard your eyes, ears, heart, and mind. Turn away from things that tempt you to believe that wealth will solve your problems. Take breaks from social media and shopping every once in a while to renew your mind and resist Satan's deception.

and be content with what you have.

Your contentment is a witness opportunity to others in our culture of discontent. Go against the culture and speak with gratitude rather than complain. Consider it a way to shine light into the darkness, which brings life and health to the places where Satan tries to stake claims (Col. 3:17 NLT).

Write the verse:

_____

_____

_____

_____

_____

Your thoughts:

_____

_____

_____

_____

_____

❀ MORE MEDITATION VERSES

Then I will praise God's name with singing, and I will honor him with thanksgiving. (Ps. 69:30)

Enter his gates with thanksgiving, and his courts with praise. Give thanks to him and praise his name. (Ps. 100:4)

The fear of the LORD leads to life; then one rests content, untouched by trouble. (Prov. 19:23)

For the world offers only a craving for physical pleasure, a craving for everything we see, and pride in our achievements and possessions. These are not from the Father, but are from this world. (1 John 2:16 NLT)

Prayer

Heavenly Father,

I praise you because you need nothing, yet you choose me to be your daughter. You share all you have with me. You are eager to pour out blessings upon me, both here on earth and when I get to heaven. You are so good to me.

I confess that I often feel jealous, even though I have so many blessings. I often compare myself to those who have more than me. My eyes are often fixed on the things of the world instead of being fixed on the treasures available in my relationship with you. I want to grow in gratitude for the abundance you have already provided me.

Thank you for every gift, small and large, you have provided me. I don't deserve them as a sinner, but because you are good, you keep providing them to me.

I want to become content in every situation. Teach me to keep track of my blessings, Lord. When I am tempted toward discontent, flash a blessing in my mind so my heart is drawn right back to you. Give me a hunger and thirst for things that will last beyond this life so that discontentment is replaced with thanksgiving.

In Jesus's name,

Amen.

REFLECTION QUESTIONS

1. In what area of life do you struggle most with jealousy?

2. When are you most tempted to compare your situation with situations of others?

3. What will you do differently this week to cultivate gratitude every day?

ELEVEN

ANGRY THOUGHTS

"In your anger do not sin": do not let the sun go down while you are still angry.

Ephesians 4:26

I did not grow up in a home where anger was properly handled. In my home, anger either was buried underground or leaked out in passive aggression. I turned my anger inward, which led to depression because my body and spirit could not contain the cauldron of poisonous anger.

A few years ago, after an argument with a loved one, God gave me a picture of the anger hidden in my heart. I have a collection of journals dating back to when I was ten years old. In my conversation with God, he showed me a glimpse of thousands of those journals, stacked up high into walls and laid out long like paving bricks.

He said that each one of my stifled incidents of anger was like a journal, full to the brim with bitterness. To get free from anger's choke hold, I had to throw each journal into a purifying fire, where God would bring beauty from ashes. He showed me green branches in that same vision, telling me that new life is possible once I surrender my anger to him.

Ironically, God is calling me to keep an anger journal right now. I simply write in it to record how family problems made me boil with anger in many different ways. When the pen touches the journal pages, rage flows out in black ink. But then it's out, and I feel free each time I complete an entry. Anger no longer chokes us when we find a healthy way to release it.

I am not intentionally keeping a record of wrongs, which is the opposite of love as described in 1 Corinthians 13. By writing angry thoughts out, I am processing my anger in a safe space, releasing it through the controlled boundaries of a pen's narrow path. Someday I will burn the journal in a purifying fire. This anger journal is a temporary journal for my healing. Maybe you need to start an anger journal too.

Anger is like fire: it can do good when controlled, but it can wreak havoc when uncontrolled. Self-control is the key to handling anger in God-pleasing ways. In the heat of an angry moment, Christian meditation can help you discharge your anger even better than counting to ten or taking deep breaths. Let's explore what the Bible has to say about anger and how we can control it through meditation.

❀ Different Forms of Anger

Anger can be handled in several unhealthy ways. It can explode, it can be leaked through passive aggression, or it can be internalized. None of these methods solve the underlying problems, and they usually cause greater harm than the original anger trigger. If we don't deal with anger, it can develop into bitterness, which harms our relationship with God and others.

Christian counselor and radio host June Hunt has identified four sources of anger: hurt, fear, frustration, and injustice.[1] We'll look at biblical examples for each of these sources.

For an example of hurt-based anger, we can look at Esau. He carelessly gave up his birthright to his twin brother, Jacob. Jacob followed his mother's instructions and tricked Isaac into giving him the firstborn blessing instead of Esau. When Esau discovered the deception, he cried out in pain (Gen. 27:34).

Esau had a right to be angry at Jacob. He had lost something that could never be regained. Plus, he faced the hurt of betrayal from his mother and brother. However, Esau allowed his hurt to turn into murderous rage, which led to even more family division.

The Bible also records fear as a source of anger. As David rose in popularity among the Israelites, King Saul feared losing his power to the young, strong, charismatic warrior who demonstrated a deep love for God. His anger is recorded in 1 Samuel 18:8.

In his anger, Saul began viewing David with suspicion. The Lord allowed an evil spirit to influence Saul, who threw a spear at David while he played the harp. After David successfully dodged the spear two times, Saul was afraid (1 Sam. 18:12). He knew God was with David instead of him. Saul's fear-based anger drove him to chase David for years in hopes of killing him.

To understand anger with frustration at its core, we can look at the story of Cain and Abel. God had apparently determined animal sacrifice to be the proper form of worship. Cain brought grains as his sacrifice, and Abel brought choice portions from his firstborn flock. God accepted Abel's sacrifice but rejected Cain's sacrifice.

The Bible says that Cain was very angry over this situation (Gen. 4:5). We can infer that Cain was frustrated that his gift was not approved. However, we can also infer that Cain knew God's preference, based on what God told Cain in Genesis 4:7. God warned Cain that sin was ready to pounce on him if he didn't sort out his frustration. Instead of doing what was right, Cain took revenge on Abel and killed him. This act caused Cain to be cast out of the Garden of Eden.

When we are angry due to injustice, we reflect the heart of God, who is perfectly just. Jacob had worked for Laban for many years, though Laban had tricked him many times. When Jacob wanted to go out on his own, Laban falsely accused him of not following all the requirements. Jacob became angry and rebuked Laban, mentioning the injustice (Gen. 31:36–42). Laban finally backed down and made a peace covenant with Jacob.

Our anger will lead either to murderous desires or to peaceful solutions. When you learn to identify the source of your anger, you can direct it in a healthier direction. But if you refuse to control it, your anger will threaten to dominate you.

❋ GOD'S ANGER

Anger itself is not wrong or sinful. God showed his anger in many different instances, and since God is holy, anger cannot be wrong when handled correctly.

Have you ever exploded in anger? No matter how angry we feel, our anger can't compare with God's anger. He is the only one who has the right to explode (Ps. 76:7 NLT). When the final judgment comes, we will see it in its spectacular glory.

God is angriest when we refuse to accept the relationship he offers. He was angry at the ancient Israelites for this sin. In his righteous anger, he forced them to wander in the wilderness for forty years before they reached the Promised Land (Ps. 95:10). He gets angry at people today for forsaking relationship with him.

Yet anger is not God's defining characteristic. Because God loves us so much, he doesn't stay angry with us. He chooses to show us mercy and love instead of wrath. Since we are his chosen people, he pardons our sins and forgives our trespasses (Mic. 7:18).

Jesus was angry with the Pharisees for their hard hearts. Though Jesus had no sin in him, the Pharisees continued to watch him for mistakes so that they could arrest him (Mark 3:4–6). His anger toward their unreasonable actions was valid. We must ask God to remove suspicious and judgmental Pharisee-like thoughts from our minds.

Jesus also got angry at people who exchanged money in the temple courts (John 2:13–16). When we think Jesus showed only love, we need to meditate on this passage. His righteous anger drove him to decisive action. Jesus actively controls when and how he shows his anger. We can follow his example of handling injustice-based anger.

�֍ Handling Anger through Meditation

Over time, key Bible verses have helped me manage my anger in God-pleasing ways. I now know to go to God first when I feel angry. He can help me sort out my angry feelings better than anyone else.

I've also learned to pick the right times to confront others. It's not wise to talk about my angry feelings when I'm tired, no matter how justified I feel. Sometimes I pray and journal at night before confronting the next morning with a clearer mind. Other times, prayer and journaling teach me to let my anger go and work it out with God alone.

You'll need to pray over these verses and ask God to show you how to apply them when angry thoughts arrive. He may lead you to apply them differently in various situations. A close dependence upon God is key to managing your angry thoughts.

Remember that anger is *always* a call to action. Sometimes the action is simply prayer. Other times you must confront. Don't let it simmer inside, leak out in passive aggression, or explode. Ask yourself what feeling lies underneath your anger and deal with that first. Then proceed where God leads you.

Ephesians 4:26–27 is an excellent meditation verse for help in handling anger.

> *"In your anger do not sin"*

Here, God shows us that anger itself is not sinful. However, we must practice self-control by refusing to sin when we feel angry. This requires prayer, practice, and meditation as soon as you feel angry.

Do not let the sun go down while you are still angry

This passage contains a principle, not a strict law. It means to take care of things as soon as possible when you feel angry. I have learned through experience that most problems are better handled in the daytime, within twenty-four hours of their inception. However, if you sense God wants you to handle the issue before bedtime, pray for extra self-control.

and do not give the devil a foothold.

When you deal with your anger as quickly as possible, you clear your mind of spaces where Satan can start building a stronghold. The longer you put off a necessary confrontation, the more opportunity you give him to take over space in your thought life. When I apply this verse to my long-held grudges, I see that my reluctance to deal with anger created a foothold for Satan. As soon as you can, go to God for help in handling your hurt, fear, frustration, and injustice.

Write the verse:

_____
_____
_____
_____
_____

Your thoughts:

_____
_____
_____
_____
_____

❀ Pursuing Self-Control

Of all the fruits of the spirit listed in Galatians 5:22–23, self-control is often the hardest one for me to bear, particularly when it comes to anger. I will always be tempted to smother my anger rather than risk confrontation. You may be tempted to let your anger explode without practicing restraint or leak out in passive aggression rather than facing it straight on. We all need the Holy Spirit's help to gain more self-control in our lives when we are angry, whatever our tendencies may be.

You can catch angry thoughts in a self-control net so that you learn to respond rather than react in a heated moment. Meditate on self-control verses so that you'll be ready the next time your temper flares.

When we are provoked, angry thoughts will naturally enter our minds. But we choose whether to let them enter our hearts. We must guard our hearts against angry thoughts (Prov. 4:23). With God's help, we can capture the thoughts and examine them, then calmly deal with the root problem. If we allow angry thoughts in our hearts, bitterness will destroy our peace.

Anger is often linked to impatience. Proverbs 16:32 makes it clear that God sees no value in uncontrolled anger or impatience. To become more Christlike, we must practice both patience and self-control in angry moments. These fruits of the spirit are more important to God than venting our anger or winning an argument.

A person who lacks self-control is like a city with broken-down walls (Prov. 25:28). This powerful word picture shows us the state of our minds when we fail to apply self-control to our anger. Letting our angry thoughts simmer, leak out, or explode erodes our protective walls and gives Satan easy access to strongholds. Pray that God will help you control your anger so that your mind is strong and healthy.

I need grace and self-control in a particular area. I have a terrible habit of cursing, but only when I'm angry. I'm praying that God will give me more self-control when I'm tempted to curse in anger because I don't want blessings and curses to keep pouring out of my mouth (James 3:7–10 NLT). This has been one of Satan's longtime footholds, and I'm being more self-controlled now. Psalm 141:3 is another verse that can help us watch what we say when we get angry.

Set a guard over my mouth, LORD

All of us have said something we regret when we were angry. This verse can be a guard over your mouth at the first sign of anger. Memorize it and call it to mind when your anger is triggered.

keep watch over the door of my lips.

Your lips can be the door to let out uncontrolled anger or the gate through which restrained words deliver blessings. God is willing to guard what you say when you allow him to reign over your thought life.

Write the verse:

_____

_____

_____

_____

_____

Your thoughts:

_____

_____

_____

_____

_____

❀ MORE MEDITATION VERSES

An angry person stirs up conflict, and a hot-tempered person commits many sins. (Prov. 29:22)

Get rid of all bitterness, rage and anger, brawling and slander, along with every form of malice. (Eph. 4:31)

Look after each other so that none of you fails to receive the grace of God. Watch out that no poisonous root of bitterness grows up to trouble you, corrupting many. (Heb. 12:15 NLT)

My dear brothers and sisters, take note of this: Everyone should be quick to listen, slow to speak and slow to become angry, because human anger does not produce the righteousness that God desires. (James 1:19–20)

Prayer

Heavenly Father,

I praise you for being slow to anger. You have every reason to be angry for the many times I have disobeyed you. But you are full of mercy and grace. I praise you for overlooking my sins for the sake of your Son, Jesus Christ.

I confess that angry thoughts have flared through my mind without examination. Sometimes I smother my anger. At other times I leak it out. Still other times, I explode. Some angry incidents are now grudges. I need your cleansing Spirit to wash away the negative effects of anger from my heart.

Thank you for giving me examples in your Word of how to handle anger in the proper way. Jesus, I want to become more like you, acting in anger only when it is righteous and necessary.

Bear the fruit of self-control in my thought life, Lord. The next time angry thoughts fly through my mind, help me stop and examine the root problem. Help me control my thoughts, words, and actions with the guidance of your Holy Spirit.

In Jesus's name,
Amen.

Reflection Questions

1. What do you do with your anger: smother, leak, or explode? Why?

2. What is the feeling that underlies your most frequent anger trigger? How will you handle it differently next time?

3. In which situation will you benefit most from practicing self-control?

Twelve

Unforgiving Thoughts

Bear with each other and forgive one another if any of
you has a grievance against someone. Forgive as the
Lord forgave you.

Colossians 3:13

One hot and sticky summer afternoon when I was eleven,
I was alone with my dad's second wife. I never called her
my stepmother because the painful memories were too
giant to overcome. We kept our distance from one another most
of the time.

She and I were baking zucchini bread and canning tomatoes in
the cool air conditioning. Since I loved projects, I happily shredded
zucchini, chopped walnuts, and peeled tomatoes in silence. As long
as we didn't have to talk, I felt fine in her presence. Even though my
top love language is quality time and conversation, I turned away
from connection with her. For several quiet hours, my thought life
hummed with activity while we worked in tandem.

Try as I might, I couldn't resist watching my negative memory
parade. The memories lined up in chronological order and marched
through my mind. I remembered the night my dad didn't come
home because he was with her. I recalled walking up the aisle as
a brokenhearted flower girl at their wedding a few months later,
wishing I could hide from everyone's pitying stares. One by one,
I recounted the hard situations and mean comments. Everyone in
my family seemed to be set against her, including me.

For the first time, I saw her in a different light that day. She was just another mom canning tomatoes from her garden in the August heat so that she could feed her family spaghetti and chili all winter long. Food to feed me too.

My parade of thoughts was fueled by unforgiveness. Though I had learned about forgiveness in church and school, I hadn't learned how to do it in my family. We were all holding grudges against this woman. It was hard to see why we should drop them because she would likely hurt us again. As the water came to a boil for canning, my indignant feelings of unforgiveness bubbled up. Though I wanted a release from their pressure, I tamped my feelings down while I wiped the glass jar rims clean. As a girl about to start junior high school, the feelings were simply too much for me to sort out.

God planted a seed of compassion in my heart that day. It was like a tomato seed that slipped down into the dark space between the stove and cabinets. The seed received the light of God's love after many years of being trapped in darkness. Today, I harbor no hard feelings toward her. When I see her, I sincerely give her a hug and speak with her in genuine appreciation. The process of forgiving her took an enormous amount of thought life transformation. If it's possible for me, it's possible for you too.

❀ Why Forgiveness Is So Hard

All of us have pockets of unforgiveness in our thought lives. It can be related to a family member, bully, friend, boyfriend, church leader, or stranger. It can even be related to an entity like a school or company. You may even harbor unforgiveness against God himself. Like Matthew West's truth-filled song says, forgiveness is something we'd rather avoid. Yet it puts a heavy strain on our relationships with God and others.

Why is it so hard to forgive? Because it feels like letting someone off the hook. It's human nature to seek fairness when wrong occurs. You hit me; I hit you back. Then we're even, right? Not according to God. He wants us to take the highest road possible. Jesus doesn't only want us to let go of our desire for revenge. He also wants us to show our offenders compassion and kindness. This position requires a thought life overhaul because Satan makes it all too easy to replay our offenses in an endless parade, every hour of every day.

"But you don't know my story," you say. All of us have one of those ace-in-the-hole stories of a person who wounded us or one of our loved ones big—and I mean *big*—time. I feel this myself.

I'm thinking of someone who committed acts of domestic violence against my loved one. Yet this person may never receive a government-enforced consequence for their horrible actions. Forgiveness does not naturally rise in me when I type out these sentences. A white-hot substance known as vengeance boils up from a volcano of unforgiving thoughts in my mind. When this volcano erupts, Satan throws a party complete with chocolate cake and confetti to entice me to return for more.

Jesus is standing in my mind's battlefield right now. He's looking at the burning lava that spills out from my volcano. It is headed toward my feet, threatening to burn and scar me. He is not asking me to pretend it's not there. He is asking me permission to use his special heavenly tools to remove it.

When I ask Jesus why he could possibly want this hot, destructive mess, he answers me with a question: "Why do *you* want to hold on to it?"

The lava of unforgiveness is close enough now that I can feel its radiant heat near my ankles. Jesus is giving me a choice I don't deserve because he's the only one capable of delivering perfect justice to the perpetrator.

"Take it, Jesus," I say with tears in my voice. "I can't handle it anyway. It will kill me."

Then he uses his supernaturally strong tools to scoop it up while smiling broadly at me. "I'm proud of you," he says. "You were never intended to hold this. Let me handle it, beloved."

You must have faith to believe God can handle vengeance better than you. Forgiveness *is* letting someone off the hook. But it is also choosing to put the person on God's hook and then walking away in peace, trusting him to hand out justice in his perfect timing. It's also trusting God to grant mercy if he thinks that's best.

There's another reason forgiveness is so hard. Deborah Smith Pegues writes, "I believe when we have been damaged, deprived, or disadvantaged by another, we instinctively want to be compensated for our loss."[1] Are you looking for an apology, reward, or refund from your offender? The hard truth is that you may never receive what you deserve from them. Forgiveness is being satisfied with receiving God himself rather than waiting for your offender to make things right.

Unforgiveness can be a major block in our relationship with God. R. T. Kendall writes in *Total Forgiveness*, "Unless we are walking in a state of forgiveness toward others, we cannot be in an intimate relationship with God."[2] When you read Matthew 6:14–15, look at it through the lens of this quote. Remember that the quality of your relationship with God has a direct link to the amount of unforgiveness in your heart. Let Jesus remove it for you, so you can walk in peace with him.

❊ HOW MEDITATION HELPS YOU WITH FORGIVENESS

Perhaps no other area of your thought life will benefit more than repeated focus on God's Word than forgiveness. This is not an overnight process. However, with regular effort, forgiveness can become a way of life just like meditation.

First, you must admit that you have unforgiveness toward an offender. You can use Psalm 19:12 as a meditation verse to reveal your lava-laden places. When God helps reveal them, ask him to remove them for you.

God removes our sins from sight, further than any eye can see. Our sins are as far away as the east is from the west (Ps. 103:12). God wants us to put the offenses of others far away too. He doesn't ask you to forget those wrongs because they are stories he can use for your good. But he will empower you to release the hold those wrongs have over you and let them stay in the past.

Even in his most painful moments, Jesus modeled forgiveness. While the Roman soldiers prepared to nail him on the cross, he asked God to forgive them (Luke 23:34). Though they certainly didn't deserve forgiveness, he was willing to grant it. Jesus is our perfect example for forgiving others even as they are sinning against us.

To walk the highest road of forgiveness, we can't cross forgiveness off a "one and done" list. As followers of Jesus, we must go above and beyond what everyone else thinks is fair, then forgive again and again. Peter thought that forgiving someone seven times was the highest road, but Jesus challenged him to forgive even more (Matt. 18:21–22). By forgiving many times over, we keep bitterness from taking up space in our thought lives.

Mark 11:25 tells us that forgiveness is so important to God that he will wait to commune with us until we release our grudges. This verse isn't a threat of punishment if we refuse to forgive. Rather, it's an invitation to highest-road faith. Be sure to lay your grudges before God when they appear in a memory parade. He will strengthen your faith as you prioritize forgiveness, as demonstrated in Colossians 3:13.

> *Bear with each other and forgive one another if*
> *any of you has a grievance against someone.*

True forgiveness means bearing with one another over a long period of time. Unless abuse is occurring, we aren't called to ghost everyone who offends us. Most of the time, we need to keep forgiving rather than running away.

Forgive as the Lord forgave you.

Forgiving as God forgives us requires regular reflection. When you consider the many sins you've committed and reflect on how God has forgiven you, you'll feel a sense of relief. When you release an offender through forgiveness, you'll experience the same relief.

Write the verse:

_____
_____
_____
_____
_____

Your thoughts:

_____
_____
_____
_____
_____

❁ PURSUING COMPASSION

One of the guideposts on the highest road of forgiveness is compassion for your offender. Compassion requires you to put your desire for vengeance aside as you research the reasons your offender acted the way he or she did. Most likely, your offender acted from a position of hurt. Compassion doesn't excuse the bad behavior, but it can expand your understanding and keep the volcano from erupting in your thought life.

God offers compassion to every single person, even those who will never accept him (Ps. 145:9). You are also called to offer compassion and forgiveness to everyone who offends you, without exception. When you grasp this truth about God's character through meditation, you will understand why forgiveness needs to be a high priority in your thought life.

Again and again, God offers compassion to us. He keeps delivering us from our sins and shows us compassion with every rescue mission (Neh. 9:28). When we forgive seventy-seven times rather than only seven times, we must offer compassion that many times as well.

God shows compassion to us within a close, loving relationship. He is like a loving father with a young child who made a mistake (Ps. 103:13). Whenever you can show compassion in a relationship, take that route. If that isn't possible, you can still offer compassion from a loving stance in your heart rather than allowing bitterness to take root.

Tuck Ephesians 4:32 into your mental filing cabinet through regular meditation. Every time lava flows from your volcano, pull this verse out. Ignore Satan's attempts to lure you with another unforgiveness party. Picture Jesus offering to remove the mess and consider how you can offer forgiveness and compassion to your offender.

Compassion is one of the valuable virtues listed in 1 Peter 3:8. Let's look at each virtue and see how it relates to showing compassion.

Finally, all of you, be like-minded

This verse doesn't mean we should follow the crowd. But it does mean we should show compassion by stepping into our offender's shoes. Understanding his or her viewpoint is a key part of showing compassion.

be sympathetic

Sympathy is how we validate an offender's feelings. It doesn't mean you've walked the same path as your offender. But it does mean you can look at the offender's path, see the tough spots, and cut them some slack. Your sympathy is a demonstration of kindness.

love one another

In Proverbs 10:12, God tells us that love covers all wrongs. Compassion results when we choose to view someone through lenses of love. You'll need to use some effort to put on those lenses, but they can make all the difference in how you relate to your offender.

be compassionate and humble.

Humility goes hand in hand with compassion. It helps you recognize that you're a sinner just like your offender. Humility allows you to stand alongside your offender rather than looking down on them or standing at a distance.

Write the verse:

_____

_____

_____

_____

_____

Your thoughts:

_____

_____

_____

_____

_____

❄ More Meditation Verses

But you, Lord, are a compassionate and gracious God, slow to anger and abounding in love and faithfulness. (Ps. 86:15)

If you, Lord, kept a record of sins, Lord, who could stand? But with you there is forgiveness, so that we can, with reverence, serve you. (Ps. 130:3–4)

Once again you will have compassion on us. You will trample our sins under your feet and throw them into the depths of the ocean! (Mic. 7:19 NLT)

Forgive us our sins, as we have forgiven those who sin against us. (Matt. 6:12 NLT)

When [Jesus] saw the crowds, he had compassion on them, because they were harassed and helpless, like sheep without a shepherd. (Matt. 9:36)

Prayer

Heavenly Father,

I praise you for being compassionate and forgiving. If you withheld these gifts from me, I would be doomed. You are my perfect example of how to treat others because you welcome me back despite the many times I've hurt you.

I confess that my unforgiveness volcano boils when I think about certain people. You know the whole story, Lord. You know reasons for wrongs that I can't understand, and you are wise not to explain it all. I ask your forgiveness for my unforgiveness, God. I don't want unforgiveness to damage me, my relationship with you, or my relationships with others anymore.

Thank you for showing me the highest road of forgiveness, Jesus. Thank you for teaching me not only to forgive once but to keep forgiving. Thank you that I don't have to generate forgiveness or compassion by myself. You will supply it for me as I walk beside you.

Help me release the power that past offenses have over me. Help me know whether to approach my offenders or simply settle the matter in my heart with you. Remind me of your example so I can choose the highest road possible in each situation. Keep my heart and mind on the obedient path of continual forgiveness and compassion.

In Jesus's name,
Amen.

REFLECTION QUESTIONS

1. When you read the story of hot lava, which person came to your mind?

2. What is Jesus telling you to do about an area of unforgiveness?

3. Which verse pinged your spirit most, and how does it inspire you to offer forgiveness or compassion to others?

THIRTEEN

GUILTY THOUGHTS

My guilt has overwhelmed me like a burden too heavy
to bear.

Psalm 38:4

F or years guilt haunted me like ghosts. Real guilt over problems I caused and people I hurt. False guilt over embarrass-
ing situations and words that needed no apology. So many
guilt ghosts wandered through my mind daily that I couldn't sort
real from false. They all had accusing faces. Each one taunted me,
saying, *You're bad. You're a fake. You're fooling everyone.*

Every guilty moment had a guilt ghost attached. Satan used
my photographic memory against me, bringing up several ghosts
every day. When memories surfaced, a menacing guilt ghost trailed
behind each one, ready to attack.

They haunted me when I handled objects I had taken without
permission. The mere sight of a cheap pen or paper clip would
taunt me. *You're a thief.*

If I spotted someone after I had overshared, I froze. The guilt
ghost put a hand over my mouth to keep me from saying hello with
freedom. *You're a loser.*

The biggest, meanest guilt ghost punished me after I jumped
into infatuation's embrace to soothe past pain and felt the grip
of real guilt instead. For a long time afterward, I faced a monster
ghost who was much bigger than me, and it always won with its
left hooks. *You're damaged goods.*

These ghosts heaped pile after pile of guilt on me. No one knew I was haunted, but I'm sure they knew I was weighed down. Some people said, "I don't know how you do so much." I had to keep moving so I could dodge the guilt ghosts' insults and assaults. When I was alone and at my weakest, they did their dirtiest work.

One day a friend invited me to join Bible Study Fellowship. We studied the book of Romans for nine months. While admiring the crown jewel of Romans 8, God kept calling me back to verse 1: *There is no condemnation.*

God wanted to free me from haunting guilt. Since Jesus died for all my sins—past, present, and future—I had no condemnation to fear. No guilt ghosts could defeat me because Jesus had already won the victory on my behalf. God wanted me to see that he no longer condemned me for the real sins, and he had *never* condemned me for my words or actions that generated false guilt. He wanted me to find freedom in Christ alone.

The Holy Spirit brought Romans 8:1 to mind when the ghosts crept up on me. If I said out loud or in my mind, "There is no condemnation for me now," when I was triggered, the ghosts slunk away. I repeated Romans 8:1 hundreds of times to fight off those ghosts. Every time I spoke the verse, they shrank a little bit. Now they are tiny, like flies I can easily swat.

The guilt ghosts don't haunt me as often, though they probably won't ever completely disappear. But if they show up, I will send them packing with the truth of God's Word.

❃ THE IMPORTANCE OF CONFESSION AND REPENTANCE

I grew up in a church denomination with a liturgical service that followed a predictable pattern every Sunday. First, we sang a song of worship, then confession immediately followed. The rest of the service progressed in a beautiful pattern of readings, hymns, and prayers that drew me back into communion with God.

The value I gained from saying the same confessional prayer for many years is that I have it ready when real guilt shows up, and it reorients me to right standing with God. In the prayer, I confess that I am sinful by nature and my sins create a barrier between me and God.

I confess that my thoughts, words, and actions are wrong and that I have not loved God, myself, or others in a healthy way. I admit that I deserve punishment rather than mercy, but I ask God's forgiveness based on Jesus's sacrifice. Finally, I ask God to help me learn from my mistakes and help me get on the right path without guilt tagging along.

God's forgiveness washes over me like a refreshing waterfall when I use Psalm 32:5 for confession.

Then I acknowledged my sin to you and
did not cover up my iniquity.

In his book about King David, Jimmy Evans writes, "David was a bad sinner, but he was also a great repenter. He didn't run from God in his sin. Instead, David ran *to* God. And God forgave and restored him!"[1] We too can become great repenters, turning away from our sin and turning toward God for forgiveness.

I said, "I will confess my transgressions to the LORD."

To overcome guilt once and for all, you must use confession and repentance to reach freedom in Christ. Confession is the first half of the process, and repentance is the second half. To repent means to turn in the opposite direction. Confession alone isn't enough. You must turn in repentance and do the opposite action to be free from guilt.

And you forgave the guilt of my sin.

Daily confession frees you from the clutches of guilt ghosts. Every day, you can ask the Holy Spirit to reveal your known and unknown sins. As soon as the Holy Spirit reveals a sin from the current day or from the past, confess it and think through a repentance plan. Identify the virtue on the opposite side of that sin and find a verse for it. Then pursue righteousness by meditating on that verse.

Write the verse:

____

____

____

____

____

Your thoughts:

____

____

____

____

____

❀ HANDLING TRUE GUILT

Psalm 38 vividly describes how guilt is like a sickness to our bodies. Think of guilt like a yucky combo of a burning rash, oozing wounds, fever, weakness, and groaning.

Once, I felt that way after getting sun poisoning. My pale, sensitive skin experienced an overdose of ultraviolet rays on an Alabama beach, and I broke out in a blistering rash all over my body. While my family enjoyed the beach, I laid inside writhing and groaning, waiting for the allergy medicine to start working. If my true guilt made my physical body feel that bad, I would confess it faster for relief.

David's colorful description in this psalm paints a picture of what true guilt does to our souls. With true guilt, our souls are weak and sick. We can't recover without God's healing touch, which removes guilt and allows us to move forward.

Normally, you won't confess guilt until you feel consequences. Maybe you get grounded for sassing your parents or failing to do your chores. Perhaps your friend turns away when you have gossiped about her. Your teacher may not give you a second chance to turn in late assignments. These are all consequences that make us uncomfortable until we set things right.

When you have true guilt, you can expect the Holy Spirit to ping your conscience. You'll get more pings the more you meditate on God's Word. These pings are from a loving Father who disciplines you with consequences for your sinful actions. But he's a father who longs for you to be back in his arms.

Guilty feelings are actually a blessing. They indicate that we have broken communion with God, and they invite us back to his presence. You can meditate on Psalm 38 to decide if you're dealing with true guilt. The truth of God's Word will help you confess and repent. As you turn to God, he will lift the weight of your sin and restore your fellowship with him.

�֍ HANDLING FALSE GUILT

If you're like me, you beat yourself up over guilty feelings that aren't linked to true sins. They may be social mishaps or honest mistakes that need no confession. However, your inner critic may drag you over hot coals of condemnation for them. We'll unpack this more in Chapter Nineteen.

Satan sets out to confuse us on the guilt issue. Since our confession and repentance restores our fellowship with God, he tries to block these actions. He trips us up by tempting us to confess things that were never wrong in the first place. He's also happy when we confess true sins over and over, even though once is enough. Through these traps, Satan gains ground in our thought life battlefields.

Your mind can't differentiate between false guilt triggers and true guilt triggers. Both triggers will cause you to feel miserable and weak. The only way to break the power of false guilt is to meditate on God's Word and hold it up as your standard of truth. The Ten Commandments are a great standard (see Exod. 20:1–17). If your action failed to show love to God, yourself, or your neighbors, that's a sign you need to confess and repent. If your action didn't breach that standard, you have no need to confess. Ask God to help you banish the false guilt ghosts when they tap on your shoulder.

❀ FREEDOM IN CHRIST

Do you remember a time of feeling free, even if it was just for a day, a week, or a season? I remember playing in the autumn leaves as a child. I can smell their crisp scent, feel the warm sunshine on my face, and remember the delight of falling backward into a giant leaf pile without fear of getting hurt. On those afternoons, I felt completely free from worries. I simply reveled in the glory of God's creation.

Guilt tempts us to forget the freedom Jesus abundantly provides. When the guilt ghosts haunt me, he is right there, waiting for me to fall back into his arms without fear. He's saying, "Remember that freedom you felt in my presence? It's available every moment of every day because I set you free once and for all on the cross."

Satan wants to separate us from Jesus's presence through the condemnation of guilt. But we can stand firm in our freedom in Christ by meditating when guilt threatens. Meditation verses are arrows in our arsenal against guilt ghosts. Let's equip ourselves with Galatians 5:1 to understand freedom better.

It is for freedom that Christ has set us free.

Jesus endured suffering and shame on the cross to set you free. He was beaten, mocked, spit upon, stripped naked, and pierced for your sake. His death and resurrection set you free from sin's condemnation. Every time guilt threatens to shame you, he offers you freedom, holding it out to you in his nail-pierced hands.

*Stand firm, then, and do not let yourselves
be burdened again by a yoke of slavery.*

Since Jesus already paid the price to set you free, he does not want you to be a slave to guilt. You have a choice: Will you be burdened by guilt as if you were a slave, or will you choose the freedom that cost Jesus so much but is free to you? When the guilt ghosts haunt you, meditate on this verse and remember that you were made for freedom in Christ rather than for slavery to guilt.

Write the verse:

Your thoughts:

When we devote ourselves to God's Word through study and meditation, we find freedom from guilt's burden. As you devote yourself to a daily intake of scriptures (Ps. 119:45 NLT), God will unfold freedom's path in front of you. You can walk in the freedom of God's presence and delight in his glory. When God's Word is guiding your heart, guilt won't weigh you down.

One of the Holy Spirit's roles is to remind us of our freedom in Christ (2 Cor. 3:17). When guilt threatens, ask him to redirect you toward freedom. You can pray that he will help you find lasting freedom as you develop your relationship with God.

The perfect law gives us the boundaries for our freedom in Christ (James 1:25). Your guilt is a response to the boundaries God set not *against* your freedom but *for* it. You will feel both secure and free when you intently study those boundaries and walk a life path with God's Law as your guardrails.

✽ More Meditation Verses

But I confess my sins; I am deeply sorry for what I have done. (Ps. 38:18 NLT)

People who cover over their sins will not prosper. But if they confess and forsake them, they will receive mercy. (Prov. 28:13 NLT)

Let us draw near to God with a sincere heart and with the full assurance that faith brings, having our hearts sprinkled to cleanse us from a guilty conscience and having our bodies washed with pure water. (Heb. 10:22)

For whoever keeps the whole law and yet stumbles at just one point is guilty of breaking all of it. (James 2:10)

Prayer

Heavenly Father,

I praise you for offering me freedom from my guilt. I truly have perfect freedom right now because Jesus died for my sins. You could have condemned me for my sins, but you provided an eternal solution. I praise your name for this truth!

I confess that my guilt has often blocked my relationship with you and others. Sometimes I ignore the good guilt you give me, and my sins cause additional pain. At other times I continue to act like a slave to sins you have long forgiven or to beat myself up for acts you never called sin in the first place. Today I confess I am a sinner in need of grace.

Thank you for giving me your Word as my guide. Thank you that I can find freedom from my guilt through confession and meditation.

I need your help sorting out my guilt, Lord. Teach me the difference between true guilt and false guilt. Help me stay close to you through daily confession. Ping my spirit when I need to confess and repent. Renew my mind so I can choose the freedom you provide.

In Jesus's name,
Amen.

REFLECTION QUESTIONS

1. When it comes to true guilt, do you struggle more with resisting confession and repentance or with beating yourself up for old sins? Why?

2. What is your biggest guilt ghost for false guilt? How can you shrink it with the truth in God's Word?

3. If you pursued freedom in Christ every day, how would your struggle with guilt be different? What verse can you meditate on this week to help you walk in freedom?

Fourteen

Defeated Thoughts

No, in all these things we are more than conquerors
through him who loved us.

Romans 8:37

I've never been the athletic type. I was a straight-A student in almost every subject but a dud on the playing field. In my private grade school, where everyone was familiar with my athletic hang-ups, I was picked dead last for kickball teams. In my freshman year at public school, where no one yet knew how hard this subject was for me, I dreaded second-semester PE.

Our teacher made us take turns leading laps every day at the beginning of class. The first few weeks, this went OK because the fast runners led the pack. I could trail behind without sticking out. But I knew my turn was coming, and I braced myself for the challenge.

Around the third week of classes, the teacher told me it was my turn. I did the best I could, pushing myself hard. But halfway through the first lap, the fast runners were on my heels. They sighed and snorted in frustration over my slow pace. One mean girl jogged right up next to me and sneered, "Can't you run any faster?"

She was popular, skinny, and athletic; I was none of those things. I wheezed out a lame reply: "This . . . is as fast . . . as I can go." Then she laughed at me and urged her friends to join in. Hot tears stung my eyes on laps two and three, but I fiercely decided not to let them fall. I accomplished that goal but felt completely defeated for the rest of the class period, and even for the rest of the semester.

Everyone had seen I was no good at PE. There was no way to hide the truth. I couldn't even run laps at a normal pace, much less handle a basketball or volleyball with skill. *Why try?* I told myself. I fumbled through the remaining weeks of class, hating every moment.

Nearly thirty years later, I still have a hang-up about running. I never, ever run in front of others because I don't want to hear laughter and sneers. Even in the privacy of my own home, or in the perfect solitude of my no-traffic country road, I hear echoes of mean-girl condemnation in my mind. *Why try?* I still ask myself. Yet my physical health is compromised now, since my freshman year PE defeat still has a hold on me.

In my quest to start a jogging program without defeat, I've been meditating on God's Word while I run. I recite Philippians 4:13 out loud, declaring that I can do all things, including running, in God's strength instead of my own. I tell myself I'm more than a conqueror with God's power as I claim the promise in Romans 8:37. Proclaiming God's truth while I run helps me overcome the defeated thoughts that have held me down for way too long. When we focus on confidence through meditation, we can turn those defeated thoughts into something positive.

❀ Confronting a Defeated Mindset

Gideon is a good example of someone in the Bible who struggled with defeated thoughts. When the Israelites were tortured by the Midianites, they cried out to God for help. God selected Gideon to be a judge who would deliver Israel from their oppression.

The angel of the Lord spoke to Gideon: "The LORD is with you, mighty warrior" (Judg. 6:12). But Gideon did not see himself as a mighty warrior. He was the youngest in his family, from the weakest clan of his tribe. In those days, the oldest sons and strongest clans were honored, so Gideon was not the top pick in the people's eyes. However, through a series of miracles, God proved to Gideon that he was the chosen leader, and Gideon accepted God's challenge.

Though Gideon had interacted with the angel of the Lord, he still worked with a defeated mindset. He was brave enough to tear down his family's altar to foreign idols, but he waited until nightfall to hide from public opinion. His fears were valid because the next day, a hostile crowd gathered and demanded his death. But God kept his promises to Gideon by protecting him from harm and granting him the power of the Holy Spirit so that he could rally troops for battle.

The Lord used Gideon's struggles to confront his defeated mindset. When Gideon gathered thirty-two thousand troops, God slashed the group to three hundred men who would fight against the Midianite army. That's a major confidence shakeup! Who wouldn't be struggling with defeated thoughts in a situation like that? Yet God wanted to demonstrate his strength through Gideon's weaknesses.

With a ridiculous combination of trumpets, empty jars, and torches, Gideon's three hundred men defeated the entire Midianite army. Only God could use such an oddball mixture to produce a victory. Under Gideon's leadership, the Israelites enjoyed forty years of peace. God transforms our defeated mindsets for our own sakes but also for blessings upon many other people.

Are you facing a giant challenge with not enough help and the wrong tools, like Gideon? Are you stuck in a dreaded situation with no certain end in sight? Are defeated thoughts preventing you from choosing God's best plans for your life?

Nicki Koziarz writes, "When our circumstances don't change, we only have two choices: settle and pout, or shift and praise."[1] We can either give in to defeated thoughts and live a less-than life or focus on the work the Lord God Almighty will do through us. As Paul wrote in 2 Corinthians 12:9, "But he said to me, 'My grace is sufficient for you, for my power is made perfect in weakness.' Therefore, I will boast all the more gladly about my weaknesses, so that Christ's power may rest on me." Learn your triggers for defeated thoughts so that you can seek God's strength instead of your own. Then God will get all the glory for accomplishing great things through you.

Satan will attempt to pin you down in a defeated mindset so that God's glory is subdued. He uses doubt to keep you from reaching your full potential for service in God's kingdom. Charles Stanley writes, "If [Satan] notices you turning a fearful or insecure ear to listen to his accusations, he will open up a full assault on your emotions until you have collapsed in the dust of disappointment."[2] Through meditation and prayer, you can tune your ears to recognize God's voice and discern the sneaky whispers of defeat that Satan tempts you to believe.

❀ HANDLING DEFEATED THOUGHTS THROUGH MEDITATION

We unknowingly set ourselves up for failure through defeated thinking. When is the last time you've told yourself, "Why try?" Many of us can relate to the struggle with weight loss. It's so easy to defeat ourselves in our thought lives before we ever take a bite of salad instead of a burger or step on a treadmill. When we forget to call on the Holy Spirit for help, we will feel defeated before we even get started.

When you're on social media, you'll see all kinds of memes to spark self-motivation. But even the most beautiful meme doesn't have the living power of God's Word. Be careful with any phrase or statement that proclaims the power of self. Inspirational quotes can be useful for motivation, but for total thought life transformation, Scripture has no match.

Defeated thoughts lead to a downcast spirit. Psalm 18:16–19 compares defeated thoughts to deep waters. You may feel weighed down by shame and sorrow if others were involved in your defeat. But since

God is strong, powerful, and mighty, he will pull you up from your deepest defeats and set you in a place of new growth. He delights in defending you in front of your physical and spiritual enemies.

No matter who stands against you, God is for you (Rom. 8:31). When you feel like everyone is opposing you, consider the list of hardships in Romans 8:35. The giants of the faith have faced these challenges, and you can too in God's power and strength. When you feel like the world is out to get you, meditate on Romans 8:37.

No, in all these things

No matter how many difficulties you are facing, this verse will give you much-needed strength. No hard thing can remove us from the reach of God's love, which is always nearby.

we are more than conquerors through him who loved us.

We can call ourselves conquerors because God empowers us with his abundant love. The power doesn't lie in ourselves; it resides in the Lord of Heaven's Armies, who graciously grant it to us. You can claim that power every time you feel defeated.

Write the verse:

_____

_____

_____

_____

_____

Your thoughts:

_____

_____

_____

_____

_____

Pursuing Confidence in Christ

My daughter, the baby of our family, was born with confidence. She has no trouble saying the word *no*, unlike her mom. I'm sure her confidence is partly due to her God-given personality. Maybe it's because she grew up in a two-parent home and felt more secure than I did. Maybe it's because she's the youngest child with two older brothers, while I was the oldest of sisters. I've heard from women in similar situations that their older brothers always protected them.

When I was young, I secretly wished for an older brother who would go first and take on the responsibility. I was born a leader, but I didn't always want to be one. I struggled with confidence even into my adult years. I had a toxic relationship with passivity and people-pleasing, which often set me up for defeat. After much suffering, I learned that my lack of confidence was costing me God's best.

In time, I realized I had an "older brother" all along. Jesus was leading the way for me. His strength and power make me more than a conqueror. I had to trust in the confidence Jesus provided me, rather than focusing on my own weaknesses, to start living a confident and assertive life. I had to practice stepping out in faith and faced many small defeats before I was courageous enough to live the life God wants for me.

Maybe you struggle with confidence as well. Almost all young women struggle with confidence at least once in their lives. You can ask Jesus to lead the way in your pursuit of confidence. Ask him to give you confidence in what he can do through you rather than in your own abilities. Confidence in Jesus is available no matter how defeated you feel. He will transform your fears, doubts, frustrations, and weaknesses into a glorious victory through his strength and power.

When you are seeking confidence, Christian meditation can empower your mindset. It can destroy the doubts and fears that the enemy places in your thought life. I have Psalm 27:1 printed on a pretty background near my makeup counter. When I'm "putting on my face" in the morning, I glance over and meditate on it. This verse helps me gain confidence because God is my light for dark valleys and my fear-fighting stronghold. When I put on this armor every morning through meditation, I am a conqueror in Jesus with nothing to fear from Satan.

When you look for God's goodness every day, your confidence in him will grow. As you watch the Lord destroying your defeated thoughts and uplifting confident ones, praise him for his goodness (Ps. 27:13). Tracking the thought life victories he wins for you will strengthen your faith.

God promises to give us a calm, secure confidence along with peace when we live a righteous life. Righteousness is living a life of wise choices that are obedient to God's laws. To conquer your defeated thoughts, repent all your sins and make necessary changes. Greater confidence is waiting for you if you choose righteous living (Isa. 32:17).

If you struggle to pray with confidence, remember that Jesus has thrown open the doors to heaven's throne through his death and resurrection. You can enter his presence with confidence through prayer and meditation (Eph. 3:12). Our faith gives us confidence in what we cannot see but believe in our hearts, as noted in Hebrews 11:1. The more your faith grows, the greater assurance you will have in the fulfillment of God's promises. Faith and confidence in Christ grow alongside each other. As you pursue confidence, focus on Philippians 1:6.

> *Being confident of this, that he who*
> *began a good work in you*

It's common to feel defeated because your journey isn't finished yet. But God has great plans for your life, and he's getting them started now. Have faith in the promise that he has begun a good work in you today.

will carry it on to completion until the day of Christ Jesus.

Keep your eyes fixed on the promise-filled future rather than on today's struggles. Your confidence rests in God's completion of your good works, not in your figuring it all out right now. As you walk down the path of righteousness, God will give you the confidence to participate in the good work he's bringing to completion in you.

Write the verse:

_____
_____
_____
_____
_____

Your thoughts:

_____
_____
_____
_____
_____

❊ MORE MEDITATION VERSES

For you have been my hope, Sovereign LORD, my confidence since my youth. (Ps. 71:5)

But blessed is the one who trusts in the LORD, whose confidence is in him. (Jer. 17:7)

Such confidence we have through Christ before God. (2 Cor. 3:4)

And now, dear children, continue in him, so that when he appears we may be confident and unashamed before him at his coming. (1 John 2:28)

Prayer

Heavenly Father,

I praise you as the strength of my heart. No one is more powerful than you. No one shares your glory or power to save. You are transcendent over all things, including the struggles in my life.

I confess that defeated thoughts often become roadblocks in my walk of faith. I get weighed down by the fears, doubts, and insecurities that defeat releases in my mind. Because I get stuck in defeated thinking, I don't always choose the best path for my life, and my service to you and others is a fraction of what it could be.

Thank you for giving me your confidence, Jesus. I don't have to generate it on my own; I can simply trust in you to provide it for me. Thank you for providing your strength and power in my own difficult situations. Thank you for giving me the opportunity to display your glory through my weaknesses.

Holy Spirit, I pray that you would help me identify defeated thoughts as soon as they enter my mind. Help me turn them into faith-building bricks rather than the dust of further disappointment. I want my faith to grow; help me gain confidence in you so that I can live the best life possible for your glory.

In Jesus's name,
Amen.

REFLECTION QUESTIONS

1. When have defeated thoughts threatened to derail God's plan for you?

2. What is your main takeaway from Gideon's story?

3. Which verse inspired new confidence in you?

FIFTEEN

REGRETFUL THOUGHTS

Godly sorrow brings repentance that leads to salvation
and leaves no regret, but worldly sorrow brings death.

2 Corinthians 7:10

When I was in junior high, I started holding a boy at
arm's length. I knew he liked me, and I wouldn't admit
that I liked him. Still, we danced circles around one
another, charting each other's moves in secret.

After a disastrous prom date in my junior year, I was D–O–N–E
with boys. Unfortunately, Arm's-Length Boy assumed that, since I
had broken up with Prom Boy, I was available. After years of waiting, he made his first real move.

I was sitting at my desk at the front of the classroom, reading
a paperback copy of *Jurassic Park* before class began. He stopped
by my desk and asked me if the book was any good. Now, this is
the perfect question for me—I read over one hundred books every
year. But since Prom Boy had wounded me less than a week before,
I grouped all boys into one negative category: Completely Untrust-
worthy. Including this boy.

I looked up into his face and replied with a curt "Yep," which
clearly communicated *I don't want to talk to you.* He lingered for
another moment as I dove back into dinosaur world. Then he
walked to his desk at the back of the room.

The longest fifty minutes of my life unfolded next. Regret
crashed over me. The pounding waves kept reminding me how I

had mistreated an innocent victim. I considered how I could make things right. Passing him a note was too risky; speaking out in class would have been social suicide. While I weighed my options, the bell rang.

He hurried out in a huff. I tracked his head as he got swept up in a sea of peers descending the steps. Five years of dancing around the truth propelled an urge in me. At the top of the steps, I was tempted to cry out his name. But a dark inner voice whispered, *Who really wants you anyway?* I couldn't speak.

Sixteen years later, I was in a totally different stage of life, married with three children. As I considered attending a reunion, memories of him surfaced for the first time since high school. When I asked God what to do, he said, "Write." I wrestled with guilt as I typed out every memory. I filled many pages with heartache, linked to other family hurts and losses.

Those tear-filled memories led me to seek counseling. They also led me to start blogging. A lot of good came out of writing those memories. But regret was my constant companion. I couldn't shake it off, no matter how much I wrote, how hard I prayed, or how many times I talked with my counselor.

Two years later, when my grandpa died, my church sent me booklets on grief every six weeks. Every time I read one, the boy's face flashed in my mind. I got irritated with myself; wasn't I supposed to be grieving my dear grandpa rather than this boy I hadn't seen for many years? Still, God pressed me to mourn this relationship that had never materialized and didn't end well. Only by walking through grief did I finally put my regret to rest.

I learned an important life lesson that doesn't often show up in American movies or novels: sometimes you don't get another chance, and you must accept the mess you made and move forward. Though I can't go back and fix that situation, I hope God will set everything right in the end. I am no longer chained to a regretful past. I'm clinging to the hope only God can provide.

❋ The Burden of Regret

Regret can make forward movement impossible. It can feel like a five-hundred-pound pallet of bricks dragging behind you every day. Nothing is more effective at halting progress in your faith journey than regret. We feel regret over what we have done or what we haven't done. Both types of regret can hinder our spiritual growth. Let's look at both types in detail.

Some of our regrets are sins of commission, meaning that we actively cause damage to our relationship with God, ourselves, and others. When we are willfully disobedient, we commit sins of commission. Jonah acted with willful disobedience when he headed west, though God told him to head east. Self-harm and gluttony are willful sins against yourself. You willfully sin against others by hurting them with actions and words. It's relatively easy to notice the effects of these out-in-the-open sins.

Sins of omission are less obvious yet equally destructive. They involve knowing the right thing to do but refusing to do it. Usually, we commit sins of omission for selfish or self-protective reasons. My past incident with Arm's-Length Boy is a sin of omission. My other sins of omission include not apologizing out of stubbornness and not giving due to stinginess. Sins of omission squeeze relationships dry through neglect. While sins of omission destroy with ice, sins of commission destroy with fire.

The apostle Paul gives an account of both types in Romans 7. I'll list his points in single lines for our meditation:

> *For I do not understand my own actions.*
> *For I do not do what I want,*
> *but I do the very thing I hate.*
> *For I have the desire to do what is right,*
> *but not the ability to carry it out.*
> *For I do not do the good I want,*

172 TRANSFORMING YOUR THOUGHT LIFE FOR TEENS

but the evil I do not want is what I keep doing.
(Rom. 7:15, 18a–19 ESV)

Can you identify with Paul's struggle of both types of sin over-lapping? Paul's situation shows us that we aren't alone. Regret must have haunted his thought life every day after he was saved because he approved the murder of Christians before he became one himself.

In Romans 7:24–25 (ESV), Paul comes to the end of himself and finds his solution:

Wretched man that I am!
Who will deliver me from this body of death?
Thanks be to God through Jesus Christ our Lord!

Do you want to lay down the regret rope that ties you to a heavy pallet of bricks? Jesus has hope for you because he delivers you from past regrets. Christian meditation paves the way to that hope.

❊ THE IMPORTANCE OF GRIEF

I once heard a sermon by Adrian Rogers in which he described grief as a love word. You only grieve things you care about. Until we let go of regret through grief, we can't fully reconnect with our God of love and the hope he promises.

You may have heard about the five stages of grief. They are denial, anger, bargaining, depression, and acceptance. These steps often don't flow in a straight line. They bubble up in a different procession over time. But you must let them all flow to reach acceptance. God can help you reach the shoreline in perfect peace.

Our theme verse for this chapter points to grief. Let's look at it in pieces.

Godly sorrow brings repentance

As we have discussed, regret is tied to past sin. We can find healing when we grieve our wrong choices. Worthy sorrow from God turns us toward truth, grace, and life and turns us away from our past sin.

that leads to salvation and leaves no regret

When we grieve our regrets and make peace with the past, we set them free and have the chance to choose salvation. Salvation means being covered with the blood of Jesus's sacrifice in God's eyes, which cleanses us from our sins of commission and omission.

but worldly sorrow brings death.

You won't find peace simply by feeling sorry for something you did or didn't do. You must accept that Jesus covers your sins with his sacrifice, or you risk being condemned for those past sins. The grieving process includes repentance. You can't rewrite the past, but you can move forward on a righteous path, refusing to repeat the same sins.

Write the verse:

_____
_____
_____
_____
_____

Your thoughts:

_____
_____
_____
_____
_____

❅ Handling Regret through Meditation

The Bible provides us with several key scriptures for dealing with regret. These verses provide freedom when regret threatens to pin us down.

Isaiah 1:18 helps us deal with sins of commission. Jesus freely offers you forgiveness and release, no matter how serious your sin is. He will completely clean you from the sin, so it no longer has power over you. Simply come to Jesus with your confession and repentance, and the matter will be settled once and for all.

I like to apply Luke 9:23 to my sins of omission. Some past sins can't be reversed, but their effects can be felt for a long time. They can be crosses we bear for choices we should have made. I think of their consequences as the responsibility God wants me to bear. Thankfully, Jesus offers to help us bear our burdens, so they won't feel as heavy to us anymore (see Matt. 11:28–30).

Staying stuck in regret is a form of childish thinking, as described in 1 Corinthians 13:11. A mature Christian doesn't dwell on the past but takes responsibility for her actions and moves forward in God's grace. God doesn't want any of us to stay stuck in one regretful train of thought for the rest of our lives. We must put regretful thoughts behind us to grow and mature.

The apostle Paul chose to forget the sins of his past and press forward with the greater purpose God called him to pursue. With intention, he put his condemning past behind to pursue heavenly goals (Phil. 3:12–14). His testimony inspires us to do the same. When you release your grip on the past, you can press on toward a brighter tomorrow, full of hope and life.

Let me pause here and say something important. I needed professional help to get over my regret and other hang-ups. There's nothing I regret about seeking that kind of help, except that I wish I had done it much sooner, when I was a teen. If you feel stuck in regret or any other type of negative emotions I describe in this book, don't hesitate to ask your parents, pastor, or school counselor for help in getting counseling. Your future self will thank you for taking that brave step, and you will never regret making that healing choice for your mental well-being.

✽ HEALING THROUGH HOPE

Your relationship with Jesus gives you the ultimate hope of heaven. That's where regret will no longer be a burden. In heaven, we will even have chances to make amends.

Here is where I find hope for the redemption of my regret. I believe Arm's-Length Boy and I will see each other in heaven someday. I'm picturing a beautiful field that God has reserved for our encounter. One afternoon in heaven, we will walk beside each other as brother and sister. In that heavenly place, regret will have no more power over us. We will work out the past in complete understanding and rejoice in the shared love of our Savior, who is making all things new (Rev. 21:5).

Dear one, God has fields of hope prepared for you too. If it's possible to meet now on an earthly field and make things right this side of heaven, don't wait. Pray about it first and seek wise counsel. Then walk in the field with the person you hurt and show them you have repented. If that situation isn't possible or wise, place your hope in the Lord. He will either wipe your regrets away or repair them in the heavenly places.

Satan binds you to the past every time you are tempted to dwell on regretful thoughts. But God wants you to focus on the beautiful future he's prepared for you. Micah Maddox writes, "Time doesn't heal all wounds; Jesus does."[1] Through Christian meditation, you can renew your mind with hope to fight off regretful thoughts.

Jeremiah 29:11 is a popular verse because we all want to hope for a brighter future. Meditating on future-focused verses like this one can bring our thoughts out of the past. This verse shows you

176 TRANSFORMING YOUR THOUGHT LIFE FOR TEENS

God is for you as you put regretful thoughts behind. His master plans will propel you forward into hope-filled purposes.

God doesn't say we should never look back. Reflecting on the past every so often helps us learn much about ourselves. Lamentations 3:19–23 tells us that Jeremiah reflected on times of sorrow and regret. However, the majority of our thoughts should be forward-focused and hope-filled. By focusing on God's love, compassion, and faithfulness, we resist Satan's backward pull in our thought lives.

I've put hope in people and things that eventually disappointed me, and I'm sure you've done the same. But hope in God never disappoints us (Rom. 5:5 NLT). The Holy Spirit seals hope in our hearts when we believe. God will never let us down because his great love is the fulfillment of our hope.

The scriptures are our main source of hope (Rom. 15:4). They teach us God's truth, help us endure trials, and encourage us to move forward. Your daily Bible study and meditation will keep your mind fixed on the future, where hope resides. You'll find no hope in past regrets, but you will find hope in God's promises for the present and the future, as described in Hebrews 6:19–20a (NLT).

This hope is a strong and trustworthy anchor for our souls.

Hope is an anchor for your heart, mind, and soul. By focusing on hope, you can have the strength to overcome past regrets. It's a trustworthy anchor you can return to again and again.

It leads us through the curtain into God's inner sanctuary. Jesus has already gone in there for us.

Hope helps us develop a close relationship with God, where we find total relief from regrets. Choose hope to gain even more access to Jesus. He is waiting for you in heaven's inner sanctuary, where regret can no longer touch you.

Write the verse:

_____
_____
_____
_____
_____

Your thoughts:

_____
_____
_____
_____
_____

❁ MORE MEDITATION VERSES

Forget the former things; do not dwell on the past. (Isa. 43:18)

The LORD is good to those whose hope is in him, to the one who seeks him. (Lam. 3:25)

But as for me, I watch in hope for the LORD, I wait for God my Savior; my God will hear me. (Mic. 7:7)

For through the Spirit, by faith, we ourselves eagerly wait for the hope of righteousness. (Gal. 5:5 ESV)

Put all your hope in the gracious salvation that will come to you when Jesus Christ is revealed to the world. (1 Pet. 1:13b NLT)

Prayer

Heavenly Father,

I praise you as my source of hope. Because you have set me free from regret, I have the promise of a hopeful future when my past no longer has power over me.

I confess that I have entertained regretful thoughts when you wanted me to let them go. I have obsessed over wrongs I've done and things I left undone. But there's no going back now. I trust you to help me make things right, either now or in heaven.

Thank you for forgiving my sins of omission and commission, Lord. I need your coverage for all of them. Thank you, Jesus, for taking my place on the cross.

Help me choose hope rather than dwelling on the past. I don't want to be stuck there anymore but to move forward into the bright future you have promised. Remind me that you have set me free from the past. Inspire new hope in me every time I meditate on your Word.

In Jesus's name,

Amen.

REFLECTION QUESTIONS

1. What is your deepest regret over a sin of commission?

2. What sin of omission has caused you to regret the past?

3. How can hope in the future bring healing to both of those sins?

Sixteen

Painful Thoughts

You keep track of all my sorrows.
You have collected all my tears in your bottle.
You have recorded each one in your book.

Psalm 56:8 NLT

Wher depression settles on you, painful thoughts invade your mind. Each one is a paper cut on your brain, and too many at once cause internal bleeding.

The word *never* was attached to each painful thought in my seasons of depression. Satan crept into the darkness and planted never-bombs on my mind's battlefield. When I allowed a painful thought to surface, a never-bomb exploded and shrapnel flew, wounding my whole spirit.

In my childhood depressions, my painful thoughts were attached to loneliness and responsibility. Long summers as a latchkey child scraped joy from my thoughts like the dental assistant scrapes plaque from your teeth. I constantly worried about whether the door was locked, whether a stranger would invade, and whether my performance on chores was up to par. While loaded down with too much responsibility as the oldest daughter in a single-parent home, I believed the painful lie: *You'll never find peace.*

In my teenage depressions, my painful thoughts related to self-image. I binged for comfort, which packed more than fifty extra pounds on my medium-sized frame. Though I knew every extra bite would weigh me down, I couldn't resist the soothing mouthfeel of chocolate pudding or the satisfying crunch of tortilla chips. As I stared at myself in the mirror, painful thoughts spoke the lie: *You'll never be beautiful.*

My college depressions were driven by rejection. One semester, I enjoyed daily conversation with an attractive boy, and I sensed a spark. At the beginning of the next semester, he suddenly refused to speak to me. Each time I drove down the mountain for work and he drove up for classes, my rejection wound reopened. When we met at the four-way stop, he stared straight ahead. Rejection repeated the lie: *You'll never be wanted.*

My adult depressions have revolved around hopelessness. In my relationship issues, I too often ruminated on what was wrong. Many times, when I was driving on a two-lane highway, Satan flashed the idea of my veering into oncoming traffic. Horrified, I repressed those thoughts and told no one. The *never*-laced lie was this: *Things will never improve.*

Depression is on the rise in your generation. A large study found that 71 percent of young adults have experienced serious psychological distress in the past month, and the majority of those affected are female.[1] It's one of the main ways Satan is attacking your generation, but there is help for you and your peers affected by this common problem.

I urge you to get professional help if you are having self-destructive thoughts like the ones I described. If you notice your friend or loved one expressing painful thoughts, don't hesitate to call for help, because painful thoughts can lead to disaster.

When I received counseling for my depressions, I learned to let painful thoughts go by pouring them out to God. Satan wants you to keep them inside, where he uses painful thoughts to build strongholds. By meditating on verses of healing and hope, you can retrain your mind to think life-giving thoughts. Depression is difficult to overcome, but God's Word holds the keys to recovery.

❀ THE STARTING POINT OF PAIN

As soon as sin entered the world, pain became a permanent problem. After the fall, pain entered Eve's most vulnerable spaces—her marriage and her motherhood (Gen. 3:16). Women have dealt with pain in these areas and many others ever since. Our relationships are constantly challenged by pain, not only when giving birth or saying "I do."

In the same way, Adam was cursed with pain in one of his most vulnerable areas—work (Gen. 3:17). Due to sin's effects, his work became tinged with toil. Work can cause physical, emotional, and mental pain. The pain we experience in our work often flows over into our relationships, creating a painful cycle.

You can find a measure of peace by accepting that we live in a world cursed with pain. I'm naturally idealistic, so it took me a long time to adjust my expectations, but it helped me manage pain and gain peace. When I listened to others' pain stories, I realized I wasn't alone in mine, and I grew in acceptance.

The Bible tells us to expect pain all the way up until when Jesus returns. Paul writes in Romans 8:22, "We know that the whole creation has been groaning as in the pains of childbirth right up to the present time." Pain will continue to show up in creation itself in many different areas of our lives. Accepting this fact can open the door to healing.

❀ THE MANY FACETS OF PAIN

I enjoy listening to country music. When riding in the car, it's the one music genre my family agrees upon. But when I'm enduring a painful season, I set limits on how often I listen to it. Most country songs are rooted in pain. The more I expose myself to virtual pain, the more hurtful my literal pain feels.

Jean Lush writes, "There are certain painful emotions that will always cause us to suffer tension until we root them out of our lives. . . . Until we learn to control these emotions, we will suffer from incredible tension."[2] We must intentionally handle painful thoughts and emotions to experience healing.

When we ruminate on painful thoughts, we increase our exposure to pain. Satan entrenches us in strongholds by playing painful thoughts on repeat. You can break out of repeat cycles by meditating on verses that specifically apply to each one. Let's look at common painful thought strongholds and verses you can use to fight back.

REJECTION

Rejection is one of the most painful aspects of the human experience. I can instantly recall dozens of times I've experienced rejection, and I'm sure you can too. Though many people may reject you, God will never reject you. You are his special possession whom he promises not to reject (Ps. 94:14 NLT). When you feel rejected by others, God offers you comfort, affirmation, and peace.

SEPARATION

Many of us have endured temporary or permanent separations from people we love or from happy situations. Romans 8:38–39 gives us a wonderful list that proves nothing can ever separate us from God's powerful love. When I feel separated from the love or happiness I seek, I use this passage as a shield against painful thoughts.

DEPRESSION

I've learned to view my seasons of depression as opportunities to draw closer to God. He doesn't call my depression sin, nor does he expect me to snap out of it. He invites me into closer fellowship when dark clouds weigh on my soul. I can always find healing when he is near. Psalm 43:5 (NLT) says that when we feel discouraged or sad, we can put our hope in God. Your spirit will lift when you choose to praise him in depressed seasons.

WEAKNESS

I often feel like I won't be able to recover after spiritual attacks in my weak areas. But God renews my strength as I pray and meditate. Isaiah 40:28–31 holds a promise that when you feel weak, God will infuse you with his strength. Imagine a mighty eagle flying high in the sky, powered by God-given strength. That's the picture God wants you to meditate upon when you feel weak.

PERSECUTION

Have you been mocked, belittled, or excluded due to your faith? If so, the Bible says you are blessed. Many of our Christian brothers and sisters around the world experience violence and death because of their belief in Jesus. Though you may not face such extreme circumstances, subtler persecution still hurts. You can meditate on 1 Peter 5:9 to find encouragement when you are persecuted. It will help you stand strong as you lean on God to recover.

SADNESS

Sadness is part of the human experience, but it's never easy to face. Our theme verse for this chapter can comfort us in times of sadness. Let's look at Psalm 56:8 (NLT) line by line.

You keep track of all my sorrows.

No one else knows all the sorrows of your heart like God does. They matter greatly to him. Meditating on this truth can help you feel valued and affirmed.

You have collected all my tears in your bottle.

God captures your tears because he loves you. He cries alongside you when you hurt. Everything you feel matters to him, even if it seems like it matters to no one else.

You have recorded each one in your book.

Know that God's records of your sorrows and tears are trustworthy in his hands. He will limit them according to his perfect knowledge and work them out for your ultimate good. While you are sad, he is sitting right beside you and watching over you with love.

Write the verse:

_____

_____

_____

_____

_____

Your thoughts:

_____

_____

_____

_____

_____

✿ SEEKING GOD'S COMFORT THROUGH MEDITATION

When painful thoughts enter your mind, you need comfort right away. God's comfort will strengthen you after you are wounded. Christian meditation is your medicine when painful thoughts affect you.

Psalm 119:50 tells us that God's promises are our main source of comfort when we are afflicted. The comfort of God's Word is less like a fuzzy blanket and more like a fortifying strengthener for your faith. When you go to God's Word first for comfort, you will gain the supernatural strength you need to push through your pain.

Our suffering isn't meaningless. When we suffer for following Jesus, God pours out his comfort in showers of healing (2 Cor. 1:5). Jesus perfectly understands our pain, as described in Isaiah 53:4. His sufferings bring us comfort because no one has endured pain like he has endured. As painful thoughts affect you, draw close to the wounded healer.

When you struggle with painful thoughts, you have a choice: Will you let your heart be troubled or not? John 14:1 tells us we can believe in God rather than dwell on troubles. In our painful moments, we can shut trouble out of our hearts by believing in and meditating upon God's promises to comfort, heal, and strengthen us.

Our sufferings have a time limit—and that's great news. We won't suffer forever, and someday our painful thoughts will be replaced with unimaginable glory (Rom. 8:18). We can find great hope in Revelation 21:4, which holds the promise of heaven, where pain can no longer affect us. When Satan shoves a painful sword into your thought life, meditate on this verse and remember this promise.

❃ THE PROMISE OF HEALING

Healing may seem impossible when you are drowning in painful thoughts. I understand what it's like to lose hope in broken relationships and difficult situations. When painful thoughts start whispering lies to me, I let my tears fall while I go to God in prayer. Then I claim God's promises in meditation, call on trusted friends for help, and practice good self-care. A full night's sleep also works wonders for my comfort level. These steps can help you overcome painful thoughts too.

Healing is possible if you seek God first. Consider your painful thoughts calls to action. God wants you to run to him like you would run to the first aid kit if you were bleeding. Healing verses like Isaiah 58:8 (NLT) can help you find relief in your painful moments. Let's take a closer look.

Then your salvation will come like the dawn

When our thoughts are focused outward, on God and others, instead of ruminating on pain, God rescues us from our painful thought patterns. His salvation will arrive just as predictably as the sunrise. You can trust him to rescue you.

and your wounds will quickly heal.

Your wounds will heal faster if you go to God first. Painful thoughts like to center back on themselves in circle after circle. God will break those painful cycles when you ask him for healing. With his help, you will see your wounds heal before your eyes.

Your godliness will lead you forward

When you pursue godliness rather than self-pitying thought patterns, God will lift you up out of painful thinking. It takes godly character, courage, and strength to choose healing over painful thoughts. God will help you move forward as you obey his laws and choose the right path.

and the glory of the LORD will protect you from behind.

You can draw comfort from the fact that, while you are healing, God is protecting you on all sides. His own glorious presence protects you on the front, sides, and back to keep you from further hurt. You can rest in his protection.

Write the verse:

_____

_____

_____

_____

_____

Your thoughts:

_____

_____

_____

_____

_____

�֍ MORE MEDITATION VERSES

LORD my God, I called to you for help, and you healed me. (Ps. 30:2)

I am suffering and in pain. Rescue me, O God, by your saving power. (Ps. 69:29 NLT)

He heals the brokenhearted and binds up their wounds. (Ps. 147:3)

As a mother comforts her child, so will I comfort you. (Isa. 66:13a)

Heal me, LORD, and I will be healed; save me and I will be saved, for you are the one I praise. (Jer. 17:14)

Blessed are those who mourn, for they will be comforted. (Matt. 5:4)

Prayer

Heavenly Father,

I praise you as my Healer. Your healing is better than medicine or bandages. It heals my heart in places no one else sees. I love that perfect healing is possible with you.

I confess that I have allowed painful thoughts to repeat in my mind without turning to you for help. When I steep myself in painful thoughts, I allow Satan to gain power over me. I want to receive comfort by taking my pain to you. I believe the best healing is available only in relationship with you.

Thank you for suffering on my behalf Jesus. Thank you for affirming all my hurts. I'm thankful I can come to you anytime and share all my pain with you. Nothing is too small for your notice or too large for you to handle, and I am grateful for the strength you give.

Teach me to immediately cry out to you when painful thoughts enter my mind. Help me turn to you first rather than toward any other source of comfort. Provide full healing for my hurts. Give me the hope of a painless eternity with you in heaven.

In Jesus's name,
Amen.

REFLECTION QUESTIONS

1. What is the source of your current painful thoughts?

2. Which verse in this chapter brought you the most comfort?

3. Where do you most need the Lord's healing in your thought life?

SEVENTEEN

IMPURE THOUGHTS

Create in me a pure heart, O God, and renew a
steadfast spirit within me.

Psalm 51:10

When I was a teen in the 1990s, impure images were available mostly in print. This was before the internet made these images so easily accessible. But I still had access to them, even as a rule-following Christian college student who attended church every week.

On holiday breaks, I came home and relaxed by flipping through catalogs from the mailbox. I pretended to fill my future kitchen with Williams-Sonoma products. I imagined myself in the French countryside, dressing up my home with Ballard Designs decor. When I looked through the Spiegel catalog, I was a fashionista with a closet full of designer clothing.

The Victoria's Secret catalog was my private pleasure. The lingerie was lovely, and the women were gorgeous. Which silky thing would look pretty on me? Which color of lace would I choose? The seductive photos drew me into a velvet-lined trap. Soft porn held me captive for forty-five minutes I couldn't ever get back, and worse, the images were permanently secured in my mind.

I'm not proud to talk about this struggle. But I'm going first today because this is an enormous problem for your generation. You're not alone in your struggle with impure thoughts. In fact,

56 percent of teen girls have sought out porn at least once, and one-third of teen girls seek it out weekly.[1]

Thanks to smartphones, porn is at our fingertips whether we seek it or not. When I was searching for a Bible app, an app icon in the list showed a girl wearing stilettos, bending over to display her generous cleavage. No one would expect to find porn in a Bible app search, but it was there all the same. Satan's favorite hook for your generation is impure images. He'll lay them wherever he wants to get your thoughts latched onto impurity.

Once, I was watching a YouTube video for a Proverbs 31 Ministries online Bible study. When the video stopped, the multipaned screen that always pops up at the end held a magnet for my eyes. It was an avatar of a young woman with short, dark hair and pale skin. Her black eyes looked to her left. As an art major, I was trained to move a viewer's eye through the high contrast between black and white, and that's just what was going on. The teen girl's eyes pointed to the next pane on the right, where Satan wanted me to look. There I saw a graphic sex scene in miniature. Right after a Bible study video!

This was no coincidence: Satan knew *exactly* what he was doing. He works through algorithms and evil people to place dirty images in the same searches for God's truth. Friend, if we don't learn to guard our minds against impurity, we will get sucked into a deadly trap without even trying. Since our flesh always leans toward impurity, our willpower isn't strong enough to fight these temptations. This may be the most important thought life area for your generation to fight back with Christian meditation.

Our impure thoughts are invisible, but they weaken and sicken us while leading us on a path to destruction. In our sex-saturated culture, even Christian girls secretly struggle with lust. It's still something I have to intentionally fight myself. In our pleasure-driven world, we must use God's Word to filter impure thoughts from our minds, since temptation comes at us nonstop. Christian meditation is one of the most effective tools for removing impurity from our thoughts.

✽ DEALING WITH IMPURE THOUGHTS

To deal with impure thoughts, we must first admit the truth. We are all prone to sin as imperfect humans, and we have eyes that are drawn to impure images. Starting today, promise God you'll be honest with him when impure thoughts enter your mind. The temptation itself is not a sin, so don't feel guilty for being tempted. However, lust is waiting one step away from the temptation. You must immediately surrender your thoughts to God every time impure images enter. Over time you'll notice a drastic drop in the battle you face.

Next, you must discover your triggers and take deliberate steps to avoid them. Consider which lures tempt you most. Is it a certain social media account, YouTube channel, or internet site? You can block accounts that pose a problem or install a filtering system on your phone. Perhaps a television show, movie, or video game hooks you with racy images. Delete accounts and ask your parents for help. Confessing your sin to God and others will help you wriggle free from porn's alluring hooks. Realize that the stronger your temptations, the more dramatic changes may be necessary to stop impurity's flow into your thought life.

A practical way to keep impure thoughts from entering your mind is to "bounce" your eyes away from the trigger, just as you would pull your hand away from a hot stove.[2] Immediately looking away instead of lingering on the image breaks the chemical rush of pleasure in your brain that makes you crave more impurity. If sexy internet images pop up in your view, force your eyes to bounce away in the same second. When you bounce your eyes, Satan's hooks will be deflected, and you will obey God's command to "flee from sexual immorality," as described in 1 Corinthians 6:18.

How do you feel when you are tempted to look at impure images? In my case, it's loneliness. You can find healthy ways to deal with your base feeling to avoid impure thoughts. My ways of fighting back include taking a walk, calling a friend, listening to praise music, or busying myself with a project like cooking or gardening. You need to have a list of healthy activities to which you can redirect your focus if impure thoughts are a frequent temptation. Pray about your base feeling and seek God's comfort and strength so impure thoughts aren't as tempting in your moments of weakness.

One way too many teen girls get caught in a trap of impure thoughts is to sext naked pictures to boys. If you've been asked to do this, realize Satan himself is baiting the hook more than the boy. Remember you have the power of the Holy Spirit living in you. He grants you both permission and courage to say *no*. Your body is a temple of the Holy Spirit, as described in 1 Corinthians 6:19–20. Since God bought you at the high price of Jesus's innocent death, you are greatly valued. He calls you to honor him with your beautiful body made in God's own image. Don't allow anyone to lure you into that trap.

When you commit to removing impure thoughts from your mind, or to stop tempting others to entertain impure thoughts, remember that Satan will double or triple his assaults to try to keep you hooked. Expect temptations to increase when you start renewing your mind. Tearing down the impurity stronghold requires an extra boost of spiritual strength, which you can find in Christian meditation.

❀ HANDLING IMPURITY WITH MEDITATION

Donna Partow writes, "The more we see God for who he is—the more we behold his holiness—the more we will see our *need of cleansing*."[3] By meditating on God's holiness in contrast to our impurities, we can come clean in his presence.

God invites us to draw close to him. But he wants our hearts and minds to be purified before we seek a deeper relationship with him (Ps. 24:3–4). When you guard your mind against impure thoughts, you open the door to greater fellowship with God.

Only the blood of Jesus can cleanse us from our impure thoughts. None of us can clean ourselves from sin (Prov. 20:9). Our own will-power isn't strong enough. Only a moment-by-moment dependence on Jesus will purify our hearts and minds.

Since you'll never be completely immune to impure images, you need to be prepared for when they enter your mind. Memorize the short prayer of Psalm 51:10 to use in moments when impurity hooks you. It will cleanse and recommit your mind and heart to him. Regular meditation on this verse will guard and purify your thoughts.

Psalm 73:1 tells us that God shares his riches with those who seek purity. If you want God's best for your life, you need to commit to a pursuit of pure thoughts. However, you'll need to check in with God every day about which impure thoughts need to be replaced. He sees every impure thought you entertain and knows all the base feelings that cause you to crave impurity (Prov. 16:2). Yet he offers help and healing every time you ask.

The Corinthian culture held many temptations toward lust, like ours does. Paul was concerned that the Corinthian church would be led astray by the surrounding culture, as described in 2 Corinthians 11:3. The more you meditate on God's Word, the more you will recognize God's protective voice and avoid Satan's hook-filled whispers. Let's meditate on 2 Timothy 2:22 (NLT) for three practical ways to pursue purity.

Run from anything that stimulates youthful lusts.

You can't afford to be casual about impure thoughts. We are instructed to *run* from them because they quickly lead to lust. Paul uses the word *anything* to leave nothing out. Whether it's in print, online, or in person, run from it.

> *Instead, pursue righteous living,*
> *faithfulness, love, and peace.*

While running from impure thoughts, God gives you four things to pursue. Righteous living that pleases him. Faithfulness to stay strong in the fight. Love for others rather than consuming impure images. Perfect peace that comforts your soul.

> *Enjoy the companionship of those who*
> *call on the Lord with pure hearts.*

If you surround yourself with other Christians who are pursuing purity, you will have greater strength in the fight. Find a trustworthy prayer partner who will lift you up when you are tempted. Reach out to them when temptation seems irresistible, and you'll find relief and hope.

Write the verse:

_____

_____

_____

_____

Your thoughts:

_____

_____

_____

_____

❀ PURSUING HOLINESS

God sees you as holy when you are a Christ-follower. *Holy* means to be clean and without fault, as well as set apart for special purposes. God sees you this way only because Jesus died for you and took the punishment for your sins.

Before the world was created, God chose you to be holy in his eyes (Eph. 1:4). You are like a gorgeous crystal vase because you are set apart for God's special use. When you see yourself the way God sees you, you'll see how impure thoughts are cheap substitutes for the beautiful riches God provides.

God doesn't want us to have even a hint of impurity, as noted in Ephesians 5:3. That may sound overwhelming to you. But the Holy Spirit lives in you, remember? Pray to him by name when you feel tempted. Ask him to ping your spirit when impure thoughts sneak in. He will help you guard your heart and bounce your eyes, so impurity becomes less and less of a problem.

In 1 Peter 1:15–16, we learn why God wants us to pursue holiness. He calls us to be like him. Jesus was perfectly sinless, which we can never be. However, we can make progress every day toward a holier life. Pursuing holiness in your thought life is the main way to pursue holy living. In every aspect of your life, choose holiness to draw closer to God. Meditating on 1 Peter 1:2 (NLT) can help you choose holiness.

> *God the Father knew you and chose you long*
> *ago, and his Spirit has made you holy.*

You were chosen to be set apart for God's holy work long before you were born. As the Holy Spirit works in you, your thoughts will be renewed. Your entire thought life can be set apart for God's glory with the Holy Spirit's help.

*As a result, you have obeyed him and have
been cleansed by the blood of Jesus Christ.*

Since God chose you, you are empowered to live a life of obedience. He washes out impure thoughts with the purity of Jesus's
sinless sacrifice. You can praise Jesus for cleansing your impure
thoughts through his work on the cross.

May God give you more and more grace and peace.

As you submit to God in this thought life area, he will provide
many spiritual blessings. You'll no longer live as a slave to mental
images; you'll be free to live the best life God has to offer. His grace
will cover your sin, and his peace will replace your guilt.

Write the verse:

_____
_____
_____
_____
_____

Your thoughts:

_____
_____
_____
_____
_____

❀ MORE MEDITATION VERSES

*Turn my eyes away from worthless things; preserve my life
according to your word. (Ps. 119:37)*

But now he has reconciled you by Christ's physical body through death to present you holy in his sight, without blemish and free from accusation. (Col. 1:22)

For God did not call us to be impure, but to live a holy life. (1 Thess. 4:7)

Do not share in the sins of others. Keep yourself pure. (1 Tim. 5:22b)

He has saved us and called us to a holy life—not because of anything we have done but because of his own purpose and grace. This grace was given us in Christ Jesus before the beginning of time. (2 Tim. 1:9)

Prayer

Heavenly Father,

I praise you for your holiness. There is no impurity in you. Because you are holy, I stand in awe of your majesty. Your perfection humbles me.

I confess that I have entertained impure thoughts. I'm ashamed to admit these secret areas of struggle. But I want them to change today. Pour the cleansing blood of Jesus over my impure thoughts. Create a new heart in me and renew my mind.

Thank you for giving me your Holy Spirit. Thank you for choosing me before I was born and setting me apart for a special use. Help me value myself and my purity the way you do.

Shine your light onto hidden impurities in my thought life, Lord. Help me resist Satan's hooks through Scripture meditation. Meet my base needs that lie underneath the triggers. Help me choose your best for my life.
In Jesus's name,
Amen.

REFLECTION QUESTIONS

1. What is your worst trigger for impure thoughts? What will you do to remove it?

2. What practical steps will you take to "flee from sexual immorality" in your thought life this week?

3. Which verse gave you new insight into the holy life God wants for you? How can you use it to fight temptation?

EIGHTEEN

CONFUSED THOUGHTS

So God created human beings in his own image.
In the image of God he created them; male and female
  he created them.

Genesis 1:27 NLT

When I was little, I played innocently with the girls in my class at recess. We played hopscotch, swung on the swings, climbed the monkey bars, and took turns going up and down on a seesaw. If we wanted to display our friendship to everyone, we would hold hands as we skipped around the perimeter of the playground. Friends for life, we'd proudly declare aloud, and our warm, sweaty hands were clasped in our promise of friendship.

During an intensely lonely, vulnerable season as a teen, I accepted a girl's outstretched hand when we walked around a mall together. "It's just like when I was a little girl," I thought to myself while strangers stared. She was my best friend for life, I thought at the time. But in my desperate, pain-filled quest for focused attention of any kind, I allowed a swirl of confusing thoughts to cloud my vision.

The girl and I would lie close together, touching all the way down our sides, while we looked at Martha Stewart wedding magazines. I let her give me massages in my gnawing hunger for human touch. I accepted her cryptic compliments that made others cringe. Though I wanted *nothing* more than a boyfriend (remember my story in Chapter Seven?), somewhere in my mind, I settled for a substitute I never really wanted. But when you are starving, you will cram junk into your mouth if only to fill the emptiness.

I tiptoed up to an invisible line during that season, but I never crossed it. Yet when I finally got a boyfriend a couple of years later, I crossed over my carefully maintained line with total abandon. In both situations, confused thoughts about sexuality blurred my vision and scarred God's purpose for me. If I had obeyed God's commands during those seasons, I would have far less regret in my life today.

I've never shared this struggle in public before, but now I'm putting it in a book for anyone to read. Why? Because Satan is waging a full-scale war against your generation by planting confused thoughts on sexuality in your minds. It's going to take honest talks and a lot of Bible study and meditation to fight back with God's truth, since Satan wants nothing more than to destroy our culture with lies in these areas.

As we have learned, your generation is the loneliest on earth. Satan preys upon your loneliness to tempt you to settle for something far from God's beautiful design. Whether you are secretly interested in boys, girls, or both, you need more than pep talks about purity to overcome temptation. You need to learn what God's design is for you because you are a beloved female, created for God's glory. We can equip ourselves with clear, refreshing truth through Christian meditation.

❀ DEALING WITH CONFUSED THOUGHTS

We need to go back to the beginning of the Bible to start this discussion. God created the entire universe, and he called it good—everything in the skies, seas, and on land. But when God created people, he called his creation "very good" (Gen. 1:31). People are designed to reflect God's glory and live in relationship with one another, as we discussed in Chapter Eight.

About one-third of your generation claims to have same-sex or bisexual attraction, more than any other generation.[1] To clear up gender confusion, we can use the theme verse of this chapter for meditation. Let's look at it closely.

So God created human beings in his own image.

The wording of this verse is intentionally different than the wording for the rest of the creation process. God created people to rule over his new creation, which reflected his dominion over all things (Gen. 1:26). Both males and females were given this all-important role from the very beginning. We humans are the pinnacle of God's creative achievements, each of us masterpieces of his creativity.

In the image of God he created them

As we have previously studied, to be created in the image of God is to be created for fellowship. It also means we are given inestimable value because we are set above everything else in creation. You are worth more to God than all the planets, stars, oceans, plants, and animals combined. What an astounding truth that can inspire your praise!

male and female he created them.

Here is a crucial passage to clear up confusion. It was God's idea to make men and women, boys and girls. In his glorious design, he made us different and separate. He chose two distinct genders to reflect his glory. Remember, this was a fact before sin ever entered the world. It was a strategy without flaw. God's original design for all people, for all time. This is God's holy plan that we dare not muddy with our own faulty thinking. When Satan whispers lies to you about gender, you can always return to this verse in meditation to secure God's truth in your mind.

Write the verse:

_____

_____

_____

_____

_____

Your thoughts:

_____

_____

_____

_____

_____

✳ God's Design for Relationships

There is still plenty of confusion to clear up about relationships between males and females. We can focus on another portion of Genesis to learn how God wants us to think. In Genesis 1:28, God gives Adam and Eve several assignments: be fruitful, increase in number, fill the earth, subdue the earth, and rule over all the creatures. They were intended to tackle these projects as a team. They needed one another to be fruitful and increase in number—that was God's holy plan for sexuality. Also, in Genesis 2:18, we learn that God created Eve as a custom-designed helper for Adam. It was God's idea to unite them together as one flesh in sexual union (Gen. 2:24).

If you read the Bible from front to back, you'll see the thread throughout of God's ideal for one man to be married to one woman for life. Premarital or extramarital sex is strictly prohibited, whether heterosexual or otherwise. In dozens of biblical examples, chaos and heartbreak ensued every single time people acted outside of those God-ordained parameters.

In the book of Genesis itself, there are several examples. When Abram slept with Hagar to conceive a child instead of waiting for God's plan to unfold with his wife Sarai, they initiated a family feud that continues to this day between Christians, Jews, and Muslims (see Gen. 16, 21). In Chapter Ten, we learned about the many problems Jacob had with his multiple wives. And in the sobering chapter of Genesis 19, we learn how God destroyed two cities overrun with sexual sin and how that culture influenced a perverted plan concocted by Lot's daughters.

Satan uses many weapons to tempt you toward confused thoughts in these areas. Through television, movies, and social media, he blurs the lines between what is acceptable and unacceptable. To stand for the truth, you need to first arm yourself with Scripture. Even if you are in the minority with a Bible-based stance, the Holy Spirit will empower you to stand strong.

Romans 1:18–28 gives us a chilling picture of what God does when we fall into a sin spiral. The spiral begins with a thought life problem, as described in Romans 1:21. Depraved people know who God is but refuse to worship him and give him thanks. So their minds become clouded and dark. As the spiral twists downward, they fall into sexual sin, degrading the truth God revealed to them. This was a significant problem in Roman culture, and it is an even bigger problem today.

This passage contains a strong warning, but it also holds glimpses of hope. If we think the opposite of confused and depraved thoughts, we'll be protected from God's wrath. Meditate on the positive action words in this passage, such as glorifying God, giving him thanks, worshipping and serving him, and retaining knowledge about him. These are keys to having a renewed mind that pleases God.

❀ PURSUING OBEDIENCE

As we obey God's plan for sexuality, we will receive the abundant life God promises. We cannot afford to let ourselves get too hungry, angry, lonely, or tired because those are attack points for Satan in this all-important area. That's when we need to tell ourselves to *halt* in our confused thoughts and pivot back toward God.[2] Meditating on verses that encourage obedience in specific areas can help you turn back to him.

Remember that your primary identity is in Christ, not in your gender affiliation. Today's teens feel pressure to build their entire sense of self around romantic or sexual attraction and make gender a core part of their identities. But your identity comes from having your real life hidden in Christ (Col. 3:3). Your thoughts will be renewed as you get to know God better and choose to be like him (Col. 3:10 NLT). You are first and foremost a representative of the Lord Jesus to a dark and desperate world (Col. 3:17 NLT). Make sure your identity proclaims God's glorious design.

Learn to view your singleness as a gift. If I had seen my season of singleness as valuable as the Bible deems it, I may have not rushed to become attached. Paul tells us that single women can have an undivided focus on the Lord, but married women have divided interests (1 Cor. 7:34). As a married woman, I can testify that this is unquestionably true. Singleness is a beautiful gift of freedom, where you can develop a deep relationship with God, explore creative opportunities, and serve him with fewer distractions.

Though marriage is less of a priority for your generation, most girls will eventually marry. I want to warn you against living together before marrying, since 87 percent of your generation feels either positive or neutral about cohabitation.[3] In John 4:1–26 and John 8:1–11, women who lived in these conditions were outcasts, condemned to death by the law. Though living together is no longer taboo in our culture, I can affirm from personal experience that living together cost me emotional intimacy in my relationship, and studies have shown that even when a cohabiting couple eventually marries, they struggle to bond on an emotional level.[4] By waiting until you are married to sleep together and live together, you will choose God's best, because as 1 Corinthians 7:9 says, it is better to marry than to burn with passion.

If you desire to get married someday, I encourage you to pray regularly for your future husband. A great example of a godly husband is Uriah, who was married to Bathsheba. You can meditate on his account in 2 Samuel 11:1–13. Uriah was a man of valor and integrity. He was faithful and honest to a fault. Though he had every right to sleep with his wife, he chose to put God's purpose first (2 Sam. 11:11). This was a man who was willing to *wait*. Pray that God will give you a man like Uriah, if it's his plan for you to be married someday.

To those of you who struggle with same-sex attraction, I offer you compassion. I hope you can see by this chapter's opening story that I cast no stones at you. Know that as you pursue a life of celibacy, you are honoring God in a way he appreciates. Remember that Jesus tells us that there will be no marriage in heaven, and celibacy will be the norm (Matt. 22:30). Jesus affirmed that some may be called to live a celibate life (Matt. 19:12), and if they can accept this, they can do so with God's generous grace.

Let's focus on the benefits of obeying God in these challenging and important areas, as Jesus explains to us in John 14:23.

Anyone who loves me will obey my teaching.

God is always inviting us into a loving relationship with him. Our obedience isn't a way to gain favor with him or avoid punishment, as we commonly assume. Instead, obedience is the language in which God best receives our love. It's how he clearly sees that our hearts and minds are fully devoted to him. By obeying the directives God places on our sexuality, we offer a precious gift to our Lord.

My Father will love them, and we will come
to them and make our home with them.

Obeying God in these tempting areas is a key to deeper fellowship with God. He wants to make his home in your heart, dwelling closely and intimately with you. This loving relationship will grow closer and closer as you continue to walk the narrow path of obedience. It's a sacrifice God values so much that he's willing to reward you with his accepting and affirming presence.

Write the verse:

_____

_____

_____

_____

_____

Your thoughts:

_____

_____

_____

_____

_____

❀ MORE MEDITATION VERSES

Be very strong; be careful to obey all that is written in the Book of the Law of Moses, without turning aside to the right or to the left. (Josh. 23:6)

Give me understanding, so that I may keep your law and obey it with all my heart. (Ps. 119:34)

I call with all my heart; answer me, LORD, and I will obey your decrees. (Ps. 119:45)

If you love me, obey my commandments. (John 14:15 NLT)

*For God is not a God of confusion but of peace.
(1 Cor. 14:33 ESV)*

Evidently some people are throwing you into confusion and are trying to pervert the gospel of Christ. (Gal. 1:7b)

But if anyone obeys his word, love for God is truly made complete in them. (1 John 2:5)

Prayer

Heavenly Father,

I praise you for your perfect plan. You made me to be your masterpiece, one who reflects your glory. What an honor to be made in your image, Lord.

I confess that confused thoughts have clouded my mind. Messages from Satan, sent through my culture, have sometimes led me astray. But I want to follow you with all my heart and mind. Renew my thoughts about sexuality. Conform me to be more like Jesus in this area.

Thank you for giving me teachings to follow, Jesus. I trust they are to keep me safe. Thank you for guiding and teaching me as I study your Word and decide what to believe.

Help me choose the plan you have prepared for me. Whether I'm called to be single, celibate, or married, help me accept with peace that it's your best for me. Help me stand strong on your Word in my generation, for your glory.

In Jesus's name,

Amen.

REFLECTION QUESTIONS

1. What confused thoughts have entered your mind?

2. Which Bible verse in this chapter most challenged your thinking? Why?

3. Which verse will help you most accept the role God has for you?

NINETEEN

SHAMEFUL THOUGHTS

Because the Sovereign LORD helps me, I will not be
  disgraced.
Therefore have I set my face like flint, and I know I will
  not be put to shame.

Isaiah 50:7

One afternoon in second grade, I knew my bladder was full. I also knew I could have asked the teacher permission to use the bathroom. But during this time of turmoil at home, it felt good to say *no* to something inside, even if I was only punishing myself.

The urge grew stronger and stronger. When I gave in and raised my hand to request a trip to the bathroom, no words came out of my mouth. The teacher stared at me, waiting for my question. But it was too late. Undeniable warmth spread down my legs and onto the floor. I had held it too long, and shame flooded over me.

The teacher, whom I loved, pressed her lips together in a thin line of disdain. Worse, I heard the laughter of every single child in the classroom. All around me—front, back, left, and right—I saw mocking faces. I was the target. They were eager to pounce on the girl they dubbed Miss Perfect. The smartest girl in class even told me, "I'm so ashamed of you!" There was nowhere to hide.

The bell rang a few minutes later. My classmates went to recess, but I stayed inside with my mess. The teacher tried to teach me a lesson by making me clean it up myself. My child-sized hands couldn't wield the adult-sized mop, so the janitor had to take over. Another witness to my mess. I fished dusty clothing and too-big shoes from the lost-and-found box to wear and stuffed my wet clothes deep inside my backpack.

I would have preferred to stay inside, but the teacher insisted that I join recess with the others, including more classes that hadn't yet seen evidence of my disaster. As soon as I stepped on the playground, I sensed a suspended silence and felt everyone's eyes on me. I didn't dare look in their faces again. At the edge of the playground, I kicked gravel with my clown shoes. Why bother asking anyone if I could play with them? I told myself a different *no* inside: *No one wants you.*

We all want to fit in. No one wants to be laughed at. No one seeks to be a target of shame. We will do whatever it takes to hide our mistakes. But hiding in shame blocks our relationship with God and keeps us from receiving healing from others.

Shame is one of the biggest lies Satan sells you. He wants you to believe that not only is everyone watching you, but they are secretly laughing at you. He tricks you into thinking you're only one social slip-up away from an attack you'll never outlive. Through bullies, Satan works overtime at preventing you from receiving God's grace. God's Word can heal us from our shame-filled memories.

�֍ HANDLING SHAMEFUL THOUGHTS

I have two more shame stories to share with you, both involving music. I started playing flute in seventh grade and continued all through college, winning several awards in my state. My high school teachers thought I was so good on the flute, I'd be great on piccolo. I hated the squeaky, showy sound of that tiny instrument, but people-pleaser that I was, I agreed to it.

Then my worst nightmare came true: I would play a piccolo solo in front of a composer from Denmark, who was traveling to the United States just to hear the performance. He wrote a piece centered around the piccolo, full of fast-paced sixteenth notes. My musical skills primarily lay in creative expression, not technical finesse. But there was no other flutist qualified to perform the challenging piece. I practiced and practiced, never measuring up even to my own perfectionistic standards. What would the composer think? I counted down the days to his visit with dread.

The performance morning arrived, and the Danish composer stood before me, my teachers, the hundred-person band, a photographer, and a reporter. It was showtime, but I crumbled under the pressure. Uncharacteristically, I lost my place a few times and fumbled in silence for several measures. Everyone could hear my mistakes and see my crimson face. But at least no one laughed in my range of hearing.

My teacher asked the composer what he thought. The composer raised and lowered his hands in a measurement scale. He basically said, "Meh," but he offered a kind smile. I was relieved it was over and hoped everyone would forget it—except the visit was covered in that week's newspaper. Sigh.

In college, I took private flute lessons. My teacher asked me to perform with the orchestra for the first time but failed to tell me the dress code. On performance night, I was the only one wearing white. Everyone else was in head-to-toe black. I should have bailed after the warm-up. In people-pleasing mode again, I stayed to perform in view of everyone's curious stares. Weighed down with shame, I sneaked out an unlit backstage corridor. On the final step, I face-planted in the dark. Someone heard me fall and called, "Are you OK?" I mumbled "Yes" through tears and limped away in shame-filled pain.

Satan is an accuser, and he loves nothing more than to tell us we are unwanted, unloved, and unworthy due to shame. He will replay shame-filled moments on a highlight reel in your memory, especially in moments when you stepped out for God's glory. He wants to reinforce the lie that trying again isn't worth it because *you're* not worth it. Whether you were shamed in public or private, it's not God's will for you to be consumed by shame. He never uses an accusing tone but removes your shame with a double portion of his grace (Isa. 61:7).

Church leaders know that shame is the top emotional wound your generation carries.[1] When you experience shame, you lose respect for authority and a desire to connect with others. As demonstrated in my own shame stories, my teachers lost face, and I pushed peers away since they mocked me. But shame is on a whole new level for you due to social media.

Cyberbullying is one of the main fears that girls face in terms of shaming. Sixty percent of teen girls have been bullied online.[2] Our culture is shifting to a shame-based platform, which says your worth is determined by what people think. The desire to be praised is all-consuming, and the fear of shame is pervasive. This is peer pressure on steroids, because with one wrong move, your entire group can instantly turn on you with shame-soaked hashtags or hate-filled comments.

In this new culture, the opposite of shame is celebrity.[3] Maybe that's why so many in your generation aspire to be YouTube stars or Instagram influencers. Celebrities have the clout to say who's in and who's out. But this is the way the world's system works, which is opposite to God's system (John 15:19). Also remember Jesus had his own group of haters, who were so viciously opposed to him that they stirred up crowds to demand his death (Matt. 27:20). Jesus remained undeterred by their constant accusations because he focused on his identity as the Son of Man who came to serve instead of to be served (Matt. 20:28).

You can't bounce back from shame on your own. It will simply get buried in your mind and multiply into more mounds of shame in the dark. Shame is all about hiding, which keeps us from fellowship with God. When Adam and Eve were first created, they felt no shame, even in their nakedness (Gen. 2:25). Their nakedness was a beautiful picture of their oneness with one another and with God. But when they sinned, they suddenly saw their nakedness as scary exposure, and they felt shame for the first time. In response, they hid from God (Gen. 3:7–10). We have been hiding our shame and hiding from God ever since.

God graciously provides us healing for shame in his Word. Denise Pass writes, "There is no shame on us for who we uniquely are. God gave us all the worth we will ever need."[4] When we turn to God, our faces will be radiant as we reflect his glory instead of being shadowed with shame (Ps. 34:5). Psalm 25:3 says that no one who places her hope in God will be put to shame because he's the one true Healer. We are not put to shame when we trust in the Lord as our refuge and deliverer (Ps. 31:1). If we follow God's decrees with all our hearts, we will be protected from falling back into shame's darkness (Ps. 119:80).

Isaiah 50:7, this chapter's theme verse, gives us several points for meditation. Let's break it down.

Because the Sovereign LORD helps me

The Lord is sovereign over all your shameful moments. That means he has the widest possible perspective and he's fully in control of what happens to you. You can trust him to help when you feel shameful thoughts sinking into the depths of your mind. Call on him for rescue—he will always be there.

I will not be disgraced.

With God on your side, hateful taunts lose their power. The hard truth is that no matter how much you polish your social media feed or actions, you have zero control over how people react. Though you can't make everyone respond in positive ways, you can find healing in the truth that God will lift you from the dark pit of disgrace and shame.

Therefore have I set my face like flint

Setting your face like flint reminds me of the movie scene when Wonder Woman decides to walk across the battlefield and enter enemy territory. She was undeterred by the bullets and bombs because she held the power to secure victory. Her face was strong with bravery because her purpose was sure. Just as Jesus went to the cross with strength and resolve rooted in purpose and supernatural power, we can face our battles knowing our purpose for honoring and glorifying God in all we think, say, and do.

and I know I will not be put to shame.

What you consider a shameful moment is perhaps one of God's testing points for greater faith. Meditate on all parts of this verse, weaving them into a prayer of trust. Let them strengthen you, uphold you, and empower you. Trust that God will not view you with shame because you are his warrior princess.

Write the verse:

_____

_____

_____

_____

_____

Your thoughts:

_____

_____

_____

_____

_____

✳ CHOOSING GOD'S GRACE

The perfect antidote to shame is God's amazing grace. You can think of it as "God's Riches at Christ's Expense" (or GRACE). God's grace is so beautiful because it costs you nothing but costs God everything. You receive all the blessings a princess gets, even though you don't deserve them. Shame accuses that you are bad, but grace affirms that you are right in God's sight (Rom. 3:23–24 NLT).

We tend to take grace to two extremes, either trying to earn it or taking advantage of it. Ephesians 2:8–9 states we cannot earn grace by good works; it is a gift from God we simply open our hearts to receive. Romans 6:1–2 warns us against the casual attitude of living how we please because God's grace is abundantly available to cover our shame. Paul says we die to sin when we become believers, and we cannot live in sin once we accept the gift of God's grace. It's a balancing act—living with an open hand toward God's free gift, and living in a way that shows our deep appreciation.

Grace is one of the clearest demonstrations that God sets us free from bondage to all sin, including shame. As Christians, we live under grace instead of being slaves to sin (Rom. 6:14). We can even bring our most shameful moments to God, as often as necessary, to receive the grace he fully supplies. His grace shines best through our weaknesses (2 Cor. 12:9 NLT). God grants us amazing access every time we need a dose of grace, as described in Hebrews 4:16 (NLT).

So let us come boldly to the throne of our gracious God.

Can you imagine how nervous you might feel if you were invited to meet with a president, king, or queen? The God of heaven invites you to approach his glorious throne with confidence! You can do this because Jesus opened the pathway for you. He faced every trial that you faced yet did not sin (Heb. 4:15). Because of his perfect sacrifice, you can go straight to God's throne in prayer.

There we will receive his mercy

Mercy is slightly different from grace. Mercy is God's refusal to punish us in ways we deserve. Grace is God's gift of blessings we don't deserve. We need both to stand in right relationship with God. Any time you feel weighed down with shame, ask God to give you mercy.

and we will find grace to help us when we need it most.

You need a strong dose of grace in those first few moments of experiencing shame. Thankfully, God gives you a fresh supply of grace no matter when you need it. Go to him for the antidote via meditation. He'll remind you of your true identity in him, and grace will remove your shame.

Write the verse:

_____

_____

_____

_____

_____

Your thoughts:

_____

_____

_____

_____

_____

✳ MORE MEDITATION VERSES

I trust in you; do not let me be put to shame, nor let my enemies triumph over me. (Ps. 25:2)

Guard my life and rescue me; do not let me be put to shame, for I take refuge in you. (Ps. 25:20)

For you know the grace of our Lord Jesus Christ, that though he was rich, yet for your sake he became poor, so that you through his poverty might become rich. (2 Cor. 8:9)

But grow in the grace and knowledge of our Lord and Savior Jesus Christ. To him be glory both now and forever! Amen. (2 Pet. 3:18)

If our hearts condemn us, we know that God is greater than our hearts, and he knows everything. Dear friends, if our hearts do not condemn us, we have confidence before God and receive from him anything we ask, because we keep his commands and do what pleases him. (1 John 3:20–22)

Prayer

Heavenly Father,

I praise you for never hiding from me. You call my name to invite me to walk with you, even when I feel ashamed. Your invitation is irresistible.

I confess that shame has mounted up in dark places of my mind. Satan would love for me to keep hiding from you. But I want to know you more without cowering in shame. I trust you will always look on me with love and never ridicule me.

Thank you for your lavish gift of grace. I don't deserve it, and nothing I do can earn it. I want to treat your grace like the priceless gift it is and never cheapen it.

Help me go straight to you when I need a fresh dose of grace. Remove my shame with the truth of my identity as your warrior princess.

In Jesus's name,
Amen.

REFLECTION QUESTIONS

1. Which public and private incidents have most caused you to feel shame?

2. Have you been bullied? If so, how did shame affect you after the incident?

3. Which verse will be most helpful in receiving God's grace when you need it most?

TWENTY

THOUGHTS OF SELF-HARM

After all, no one ever hated their own body, but they feed and care for their body, just as Christ does the church.

Ephesians 5:29

Starting in junior high, I participated in an evening ritual. The downstairs half bath was my own space, a sparse room with only a toilet, sink, and lighted mirror. I studied my face in the mirror, looking for blackheads and whiteheads to attack. In the background of my thoughts, I'd rehearse the day's frustrations and unfairness while I squeezed until I drew blood.

I replayed the insults from younger kids who walked home in the opposite direction. I was their target for pent-up negative energy. Someone had to pay for their hateful slurs. Rather than sling words back at them or ride the bus home, I'd make my face pay.

I rewound my thoughts to things I didn't want to see, like a girl putting her hands down her boyfriend's pants when the teacher wasn't looking. I needed to shred that mental picture and many others. Instead, I shredded myself.

The toughest thoughts to conquer were family problems. Ones I couldn't tell anyone. Stories I wish I'd never heard. Someone needed to stop what was wrong. But instead of reaching out for help, I turned on myself. Once I cleared what was obviously imperfect, I sometimes picked at skin that was perfectly fine. I felt sickly triumphant punishing myself.

In one issue of my *Sassy* magazine, a girl wrote a question to the editor that piqued my interest: "Is something wrong with me if I enjoy picking on my face?" A shiver went down my spine. The editor said it wasn't OK, that she may be suffering from excoriation disorder, and urged her to get professional help. My insides squirmed at the editor's advice. Classmates who attended counseling carried an outcast stigma. Maybe I'd just stop, I told myself. But on my worst days, I still picked and picked while I processed my negative and painful thoughts.

Skin picking is one form of body-focused repetitive behavior, related to obsessive-compulsive disorder.[1] The most common forms of self-harm include cutting, hair pulling, and picking at scabs or wounds. These are external forms, but internal forms like alcohol, drugs, and chemicals are also damaging. Teen girls are more likely than any other group to engage in self-harm, and up to 30 percent of girls are affected.[2] Many use self-harm to feel something rather than numbness, to release inner pain, and even to calm themselves. But self-harm proves to be a vicious circle. The more self-harm you practice, the more you crave. And the results can be dangerous or even deadly.

Even though bingeing is technically an eating disorder, I also used it as a means of self-harm. Overeating isn't as frowned upon in our culture as cutting, burning, or skin picking. As a teen, I frequently ate double or triple portions. Large portions of sweets and starches felt good in my mouth and even gave me a mild high, which I craved when I experienced lonely or painful thoughts. Bingeing was my favorite method for stifling my hurt. But I hated the taunts from classmates about my weight, which began in fourth grade. To soothe thoughts of self-hatred, I ate more, even while knowing I would gain more weight and face more criticism. This vicious behavior and thought life cycle trapped me for decades.

To overcome self-harm, we must process the negative thoughts that trigger our destructive cycles. By using Christian meditation in difficult moments, we can stop the toxic cycle and move in a healthier direction.

❋ DEALING WITH THOUGHTS OF SELF-HARM

My thinking about self-harm was twisted by something I learned as a schoolgirl about Martin Luther's life. Before his life was transformed by God's grace, he whipped himself to try to atone for his sins.[3] This act of self-flagellation was extreme and not supported by the church at large, nor by the teacher who was rendering this lesson to me. But Satan took this story and planted a seed in my mind: "You don't have to worry about rejection or retaliation if you inflict harm on yourself instead of others." What I needed was the truth of God's Word to help me fight thoughts of self-harm and affirm my worth in Christ.

John Townsend writes, "What the self-attacker needs is a safe, relational context in which [she'll] be able to aim at the correct target, without fear of retaliation."[4] The longer we isolate ourselves in pain, the more likely we are to blame and attack ourselves. But when we confront those who have harmed us, we invite change into relationships. Luke 17:3 tells us to rebuke the one who sins against us and forgive them. A rebuke is a firm expression of disapproval against someone's behavior. It shows them the harm they caused so they have a chance to make things right. In Matthew 18:15–17, Jesus lays out a four-step process for confrontation. Clearly, God wants us to confront people when necessary rather than turning our confrontation on ourselves.

As a teen, I felt powerless to express rebukes to those who needed to hear them from me: the bullies, family members, and toxic friends. But after five years of Christian counseling as an adult, I gained assertive skills necessary to stand up for myself. If you need professional help to overcome a self-harm problem, there is no shame in reaching out. If I had received counseling back when

I was a teen, my life would have taken a much healthier path. Don't hesitate to seek out a counselor's advice. Proverbs 12:15, 13:10, and 19:20 state that those who seek advice are wise. Meditate on these verses as you reach out for help.

My journals were a safe outlet for my pain. I often wrote out my frustrations. How I wish I had known the power of writing out Scripture back then. I could have poured out my feelings on paper, then written out affirming verses to strengthen my faith. A good verse for your own journal is Romans 12:21. It tells you not to let yourself be overcome by evil. Satan will try to lull you into thinking that self-harm is a solution when it's actually a symptom of deeper problems. You can overcome evil with good by praying, meditating on God's Word, and singing praise songs to God.

Another powerful Scripture for your meditation and prayer journal is Matthew 22:37–40. When an expert of the law asked Jesus what the greatest commandment is, he answered in two parts. First, we must love God with all our heart, soul, and mind. Second, we must love our neighbors as ourselves. To overcome thoughts of self-harm, you can meditate on the portion about loving yourself. This isn't a self-focused, prideful love. It's loving yourself because God first loved you. Because he pours his love over you, you can love yourself and others. Self-hatred is from Satan, but proper self-love is from God. Every time you are tempted to harm yourself, remember that Jesus wants you to love yourself instead—part of his greatest commandments for your life.

One of the best meditation verses for fighting thoughts of self-harm is our theme verse for this chapter, Ephesians 5:29. Let's look at it in detail.

After all, no one ever hated their own body

Even though I struggle with skin picking, I don't completely neglect my body out of hatred. I'm sure you're the same way, no matter how much you struggle with thoughts of self-harm.

but they feed and care for their body

Most of the time, I take good care of my body. I eat, sleep, shower, and exercise. You can refocus your energy and efforts on taking good care of your body too. By eating right, getting enough sleep, practicing personal hygiene, and exercising most days of the week, you'll be less tempted to destroy your body.

just as Christ does the church.

When I think about Jesus caring for me every day, I feel sorry for the times I considered my body unworthy of care. If he says my body is worthy of care, I must care for it. I hope this verse sparks renewed thinking in you too.

Write the verse:

_____

_____

_____

_____

_____

Your thoughts:

_____

_____

_____

_____

_____

�֍ Declare Affirmations

When you're tempted toward self-harm, Satan's lies light up your mind's battlefield. You can destroy those lies with many flaming arrows of affirmations found in God's Word. Speak them aloud so that God, your inner critic, and Satan can hear each one. Let's break the nuggets of truth in 1 Peter 2:9 down into declarations.

But you are a chosen people

I declare that I am a chosen daughter of the Lord God Almighty. Before I was born, he chose me to be part of his forever family (Eph. 1:11). For this reason, my mind, body, soul, and spirit have great value.

a royal priesthood

I declare that I am a princess of the King of Kings. I am not a Cinderella in the corner, unable to fight back against the insults and demands of people who want to harm me. I am a royal in God's eyes, like Queen Esther, who fought against Satan's schemes (Esther 8:3).

a holy nation

I declare that in God's sight, I am holy. Not because of anything I've done but because the precious blood of Jesus covers me. His blood cleanses me from my sins and makes me white as snow (Isa. 1:18). I am holy, set apart, and reserved for a special purpose that Satan cannot thwart.

God's special possession

I declare that I am God's special possession. I am a pearl of great price and a hidden treasure that my Father would give everything up to hold, even his own Son, Jesus (Matt. 13:44–46).

that you may declare the praises of him

I declare that my God is always worthy of praise, and one of my primary purposes is to praise him. I praise him now for his strength, power, goodness, and glory. As long as I have breath, I will praise him as the Most High God (Ps. 9:2).

who called you out of darkness into his wonderful light.

I declare that the prince of darkness has no power over me. The Light of the World has set me free from the powers of darkness and made me a light to shine for his glory (Matt. 9:16). There is no darkness in my God at all (1 John 1:5), and today I choose light over darkness.

Revelation 12:10 tells us that Satan is the great accuser. He will tempt you to believe accusations that you deserve self-harm. But you can make many verses into affirmations of your worth in God's eyes. God's opinions of you never change. You are not worthless; you are worth more than many sparrows (Matt. 10:31). You are not condemned; you are forgiven, redeemed, and crowned with compassion (Ps. 103:2–4). You are not unwanted; you are appointed to bear fruit that will last (John 15:16). You are not simply tolerated; you are beloved (Song of Sol. 7:10). You are more than a conqueror because of God's love (Rom. 8:37). You are the apple of his eye, whom he hides under the shadow of his wings (Ps. 17:8). Look up these verses in your Bible and choose your favorite one to write out below; then turn it into a declaration in your own words.

Write the verse:

_____

_____

_____

_____

Your declaration:

_____

_____

_____

_____

_____

❀ MORE MEDITATION VERSES

I have come into the world as a light, so that no one who believes in me should stay in darkness. (John 12:46)

Therefore do not let sin reign in your mortal body so that you obey its evil desires. (Rom. 6:12)

What, then, shall we say in response to these things? If God is for us, who can be against us? (Rom. 8:31)

You, dear children, are from God and have overcome them, because the one who is in you is greater than the one who is in the world. (1 John 4:4)

Prayer

Heavenly Father,

I praise you for lovingly creating me. You carefully crafted me with your own hands. My body matters to you, as well as my heart, soul, mind, and spirit.

I confess that when thoughts of self-harm enter my mind, I think far less of myself than you think of me. These thoughts tear me down rather than build me up. I need your help to overcome them, Lord.

Thank you for being my rescuer and deliverer. I trust you will help me pursue a healthier path. Thank you for giving me many verses I can use as affirmations and declarations of truth.

Help me to not get caught up in a vicious cycle of self-harm. You know what destructive behaviors tempt me most, Father. Help me honor you in every way, including how I love myself.

In Jesus's name,

Amen.

REFLECTION QUESTIONS

1. When are you most tempted toward thoughts of self-harm?

2. Who do you need to rebuke instead of harming yourself? Which trusted person can help you prepare for a confrontation?

3. Which portion of 1 Peter 2:9 is most helpful to you as a declaration? Why?

TWENTY-ONE

UNTRUE THOUGHTS

Finally, brothers and sisters, whatever is true, whatever is noble, whatever is right, whatever is pure, whatever is lovely, whatever is admirable—if anything is excellent or praiseworthy—think about such things.

Philippians 4:8

What is something people have told you that's hard to believe is true about yourself, positive or negative?

The positive one for me is *funny.* I have an extremely dry sense of humor that few appreciate. When a handful of people have said to me face-to-face, "You're funny," I immediately deflect their comments with "No, not me. But you should meet my family." One family member is always the life of the party, making people laugh with his stories. Another wrote her dissertation on using humor at work, so that makes her an expert on humor, right? In their towering shadows of fun, I don't feel funny at all. I'd rather believe the lie I tell myself about not being funny than believe what a few others say.

The negative one for me is *lazy.* In their worst moments, a few people have labeled me with this word, and I decided to believe them. For many years, I believed this lie about myself, that I never work hard enough. Then one, two, and eventually dozens of other people said they admired me as one of the hardest-working people they've ever met. I had to stack their mounting evidence against the handful of lies a few people told me. The real truth is that I need

232 TRANSFORMING YOUR THOUGHT LIFE FOR TEENS

to take breaks more often, since I'm so hardworking and hardly ever lazy!

A few years ago I went on a spiritual retreat, which I highly recommend to you. After breakfast, I enjoyed a quiet hike in the woods. In the privacy of God's creation, I snapped wildflower photos and sang praises to my creator. However, I was secretly feeling productive as I logged ten thousand steps on my Fitbit. At the end of the hike, it was late morning, and I had nothing else to produce that day. My mind and body struggled to settle into rest mode because I was so used to pushing myself, every minute of every day.

By 2:00 P.M., my struggle was over. God's perfect peace settled on my shoulders, like the easy yoke Jesus describes in Matthew 11:30. I wasn't being lazy at all by simply sitting on a porch and watching nature. Instead, I was intentionally caring for my mind, heart, and soul by welcoming a day of rest.

That weekend, God taught me how weary I was from trying so hard to prove my worth through what I do. The lies of those who told me I was lazy were always playing on repeat somewhere in the back of my mind. I thought the only way to silence the lies was to smother them with proof of hard work. God took me on that retreat to reveal the truth that my worth is in who I am in him, not in what I do.

So many of us live everyday lives with these lies on replay in the background. We chart our steps forward based on untrue thoughts rather than truthful thoughts, trying our hardest to prove people wrong. Satan has been telling us lies to keep us off the right path ever since the Garden of Eden. He wants us to question God's best and stay in bondage to untruths.

Patsy Clairmont writes, "If we don't agree with what's true about ourselves, we don't change. It's that simple and that hard."[1] To walk on the life path that most pleases God, we must agree with the truth God tells us and throw away the untruths. While handing over the lies to God and asking him to replace them with truth, we can transform our thinking.

Every thought life struggle detailed in the previous chapters is rooted in untruth. Satan is the father of lies (John 8:44) who uses untruths to accuse us daily. He twists the truth with us, just as he tried to do at Jesus's temptation (see Matt. 4:1–11). We must learn to sidestep Satan's untruths and choose God's truth through Christian meditation.

✻ THE PROBLEM OF DECEIT

Satan will try to deceive you in every possible way. He'll cause you to question a good truth and consider a twisted version. If you are willing to settle for shades of the truth, he's just as happy as if you believe outright lies. He's like a fisherman who baits his hooks with all kinds of different lures, waiting to see which one will draw you in. One of the sneakiest ways he tries to tempt you is to question whether you are hearing God's voice or his. Since he used tricks like these to tempt Jesus, you can expect the same spiritual warfare strategies.

Untrue thoughts are Satan's attempt to get you to elevate him above God. This has been his overarching plan for all people in history. Satan was originally one of God's holy angels, but he rebelled in his quest for ultimate authority. In his fall from heaven (Luke 10:18), he took many other angels with him. They are now millions of evil spirits who heed his commands and support his deceitful campaigns. Satan will disguise himself as an angel of light to deceive you in spiritual matters (2 Cor. 11:14). But you can't trust him. He hates you because you are loved by God, and he will do everything he can to deceive you with cruel, vicious lies. To remove untrue thoughts from our minds' battlefields, we must study his tactics of deceit.

You will need to guard your mind closely against the lies of people who surround you (Jer. 9:4–6). Satan wants to deceive as many people as possible. To know who is trustworthy, you must depend on God's guidance and wisdom. Trustworthy, godly people show evidence like a strong faith, love for God's Word, a humble spirit, and an abundance of spiritual fruit. You must guard your thought life against both the deceiver and deceitful people. The best way to do this is to be as familiar as possible with God's truth, revealed in the Bible.

Satan would love nothing more than to trick you into believing someone besides Jesus Christ is your Savior. As the day of Jesus's second coming approaches, many will serve as false teachers who will lead you away from God's truth (Matt. 24:4–5). You will become familiar with God's voice, character, and teachings through daily Christian meditation. Jesus says that when we follow him closely, like sheep follow their shepherd, we will know his voice (John 10:27). By tuning your ears to hear God's voice, you'll be able to recognize fakers when they appear. Steep yourself in God's truth, and you'll protect yourself from false teachers.

Another area where each one of us is prone to untruth is self-deception. We deceive ourselves when we believe untruths about ourselves (Gal. 6:3). Our sinful hearts will always lead us into the darkest side of the "you do you" mindset, which leads us toward self and away from God. Jesus tells us that the wisest people come to him, hear his Word, and put it into practice (Luke 6:46–49). To avoid self-deception, we must practice spiritual disciplines of prayer, confession, Bible study, and meditation and engage in regular meetings with other believers. These practices will keep our hearts humble and help us trust God more than we trust our own judgment.

The more we hear God's Word, the more we are accountable to apply it. We can deceive ourselves in years of hearing Bible verses without allowing God to change our hearts and minds. A committed woman of faith accepts the entire Bible as truth and uses all God's teachings as a road map for daily living (James 1:22). The culture will tempt you to believe one Scripture but dismiss another. Through regular meditation, you'll discover the whole truth of God's Word and learn how to apply it to your life. I ask myself with every Scripture, "What principle can I apply from this Scripture?" It works with every verse if you look for the deeper meaning.

As long as you are breathing, you will be engaged in battle with Satan the deceiver. But God has secured the final victory (Rev. 20:10). When Satan is cast into the lake of fire, he will never be able to cross over and deceive you again (see Luke 16:19–31). After you suffer spiritual attacks, you can meditate on the verse in Revelation to remember that God is already victorious in your struggles.

Let's meditate on one of the most famous passages about truth in the Bible and discover the real truth it holds. Jesus is speaking to the Jews who had believed him in John 8:31–32.

If you hold to my teaching, you are really my disciples.

Jesus emphasizes the importance of studying his teachings in this verse. He wants us to know the Bible and hold tight to the truth, like an anchor in a storm. When we do this, he sees proof that we truly love him and follow him.

Then you will know the truth

This verse is often quoted, even outside Christian contexts. There are other common-sense-based truths in life, to be sure. But these verses tell us that ultimate truth is found in God alone. God reveals his truth primarily through his Word, and that's why it's so important that we study the Bible.

and the truth will set you free.

The truth that sets us free is a person, Jesus. He set us free from all Satan's lies through his death and resurrection. This is a truth that we need to return to every day because that's where we find sweet freedom.

Write the verses:

_____

_____

_____

_____

_____

Your thoughts:

_____

_____

_____

_____

❀ ACCEPTING TRUTH THROUGH MEDITATION

Henry Cloud and John Townsend say, "Like anything else from God, truth works *for* us, not *against* us."[2] We can renew our minds with the truth God wants us to accept. You can take in God's truths and use them to fight back on your mental battlefield by meditating on verses about truth.

We must start with knowing the truth about God. By studying his many names, we can meditate on the truth about his character:

- He is *Jehovah-shalom*, our source of perfect peace (Judg. 6:24).
- God is *Jehovah-rohi*, our loving and caring shepherd (Ps. 23:1).

- He is *Jehovah-shammah*, the one who is always there (Ezek. 48:35).
- God is *Jehovah-rophe*, our healer (Exod. 15:26).
- He is *Jehovah-jireh*, our provider (Gen. 22:14).
- He is *Jehovah-sabaoth*, the commander of heaven's armies who fights with us in spiritual warfare (Josh. 5:14).
- God is *El Elyon*, God Most High, creator, mighty and powerful (Gen. 14:19).
- He is *Adonai*, Lord over our lives (Isa. 6:1).
- God is the great I AM who transcends time and space to come near us (John 8:58).
- He invites us to call him *Abba*, our Daddy (Mark 14:36).

Choose one of these names of God, look up the verse, and write it out. Then write why this name of God is special to you.

Write the verse:

_____

_____

_____

_____

_____

Your thoughts:

_____

_____

_____

_____

We also need to meditate on the truths about ourselves. Since we are always prone to a love of self over a love of God, we must deliberately meditate on truths that help us discern which way our hearts are leaning. You can turn 1 John 1:6 into a prayer, asking God to show you if you are pursuing fellowship with him or living in darkness and failing to practice truth. Our tendency is to deceive ourselves against the truth and make excuses for sin (1 John 1:8). But God wants us to humbly admit our faults through regular confession. Obedience is a sure sign that you want to live in the truth, and 1 John 2:4 can help you test whether you are believing lies instead of the truth.

Regularly meditate on the Ten Commandments (Exod. 20:1–17) and ask God to show you if you are disobeying any of them by choosing to believe lies instead. Look up the passage and choose one commandment that applies to a current struggle. Then share your thoughts about the verse.

Write the verse:

____

____

____

____

____

Your thoughts:

____

____

____

____

____

MEDITATING ON THE TRUTH

As we wrap up our study of Christian meditation, we will take a close look at Philippians 4:8, a powerful verse for total thought life transformation. Paul encourages us to fix our minds on what pleases God, focusing on different aspects of truth. We will look at each virtue in our final review.

Finally, brothers and sisters, whatever is true

Examine each thought closely by taking it captive. Does it align with God's truth? You can know this for sure by studying and meditating on God's Word, the greatest truth ever known. Jesus speaks only the truth. Listen for his still, small voice in your meditation time to determine whether your thoughts are focused on truth. Thinking about what is true will help you with anxious thoughts, as you consider whether your worry is based on truth or lies. It can also help you discover the factors under angry thoughts so that you can discover the truth about your responses.

whatever is noble

Noble thoughts are dignified, respectful, and always polite for the benefit of others. You need noble thoughts to have the courage to rise above challenges. Noble thoughts are brave and forward-focused, and they will help you fight fearful thoughts. You can use them to overcome defeated thoughts because they inspire confidence in God.

whatever is right

From meditating on the scriptures in this book, we have learned that God wants us to love his Word. He longs for us to live a life of obedience that reflects our love for him. By thinking about what is right, we can straighten out careless thoughts with intention. Right thoughts also help us avoid getting stuck in false or real guilt. Right thinking sets us straight when we are tempted by thoughts of self-harm.

whatever is pure

Pure thoughts clean our minds of impure images that push us away from God. They help us honor God's holiness and inspire us to live more godly lives. By thinking about what is pure in God's Word, we can cancel out impure and idolatrous thoughts. We can also clear up confused thoughts and choose a pure way of living instead.

whatever is lovely

No matter how many difficulties we face, we can always praise God for his beautiful attributes. We can praise him for the over-whelming beauty in his creation, for giving us fresh starts, and for giving us opportunities to learn something new. Thinking about what is lovely helps us overcome negative and painful thinking. It can lift us out of the depths of lonely thoughts when we seek God's lovely, comforting presence.

whatever is admirable

Admirable thoughts choose to see the best in others. They help reverse thoughts that criticize others. When we choose to look at what is admirable in ourselves as beloved children of God, these thoughts also help us overcome self-criticism and shame.

if anything is excellent

Our top-quality thoughts that focus on what is excellent are pleasing to God. We can focus on the positives in a situation by choosing compassion over unforgiveness. We can also follow Jesus's excellent example of humility in efforts to destroy self-focused thoughts.

or praiseworthy

As with lovely thoughts, we can always find reasons to give God praise based on who he is and what he does. Thinking about what is praiseworthy will help us set aside regretful and discontented thoughts. We can find many reasons to praise God when we focus on hope and contentment.

think about such things.

I pray this book has inspired you to take your thoughts captive (2 Cor. 10:5), put on the mind of Christ (1 Cor. 2:16), and be transformed by the renewing of your mind (Rom. 12:2). I pray your mind is now set on things above rather than on earthly things (Col. 3:2). Most of all, I pray this book inspires you to "love the Lord your God with all your heart and with all your soul and with all your mind" (Matt. 22:37).

May your mind be renewed and your thought life be transformed through the power of Christian meditation.

❋ MORE MEDITATION VERSES

Yet it is also new. Jesus lived the truth of this commandment, and you also are living it. For the darkness is disappearing, and the true light is already shining. (1 John 2:8 NLT)

But we belong to God, and those who know God listen to us. If they do not belong to God, they do not listen to us. That is how we know if someone has the Spirit of truth or the spirit of deception. (1 John 4:6 NLT)

And Jesus Christ was revealed as God's Son by his baptism in water and by shedding his blood on the cross—not by water only, but by water and blood. And the Spirit, who is truth, confirms it with his testimony. (1 John 5:6 NLT)

Prayer

Heavenly Father,

I praise you as the source of all truth. No lies can be found in you. Since the truth always shines in you, I can completely trust you. Your truth clarifies my thinking and lights my path.

I confess that I have often believed untruths about you, myself, and others. Satan and others have deceived me, and I've also been prone to self-deception. The lies I've believed have distanced me from you and brought suffering into my relationships. I am tired of giving Satan power over my thought life, and I surrender my mind to you today.

Thank you for transforming my thoughts through the power of your Word, Lord. Thank you for giving me so many Scripture examples for ways I can focus on what's good instead of what's bad. Thank you for offering me newness of life and spiritual maturity when I pursue your truth.

Teach me to meditate on your Word every day so I can replace lies with truth. Help me recognize untruths before they find a foothold in my thought life. Protect me from the enemy's attacks. Help me renew my mind each day.

In Jesus's name,

Amen.

Reflection Questions

1. Which untruths do you believe about yourself based on what others have said?

2. Which untruths has Satan deceived you into believing?

3. In what ways can meditating on Philippians 4:8 help renew your mind?

NOTES

INTRODUCTION

1 Tracie Miles, *Unsinkable Faith: God-Filled Strategies to Transform the Way You Think, Feel, and Live* (Colorado Springs: David C. Cook, 2017), 40.

2 Emma Seppälä, "20 Scientific Reasons to Start Meditating Today," *Psychology Today* (blog), September 11, 2013, https://www.psychologytoday.com/us/blog/feeling-it/201309/20-scientific-reasons-start-meditating-today.

3 Kristine Crane, "8 Ways Meditation Can Improve Your Life," *Huffington Post*, September 9, 2014, https://www.huffingtonpost.com/2014/09/19/meditation-benefits_n_5842870.html.

4 Erin Wildermuth, "The Science of Putting Pen to Paper: Studies Show It Forces You to Focus," *Michael Hyatt* (blog), April 10, 2018, https://michaelhyatt.com/science-of-pen-and-paper/.

CHAPTER ONE

1 Bill and Pam Farrel, *Men Are like Waffles, Women Are like Spaghetti* (Eugene, OR: Harvest House, 2001), 13.

CHAPTER TWO

1 Tracie Miles, *Unsinkable Faith: God-Filled Strategies to Transform the Way You Think, Feel, and Live* (Colorado Springs: David C. Cook, 2017), 161.

CHAPTER THREE

1 Julia Menasce Horowitz and Nikki Graf, "Most U.S. Teens See Anxiety and Depression as a Major Problem among Their Peers," Pew Research Center, February 20, 2019, https://www.pewsocialtrends.org/2019/02/20/most-u-s-teens-see-anxiety-and-depression-as-a-major-problem-among-their-peers/.
2 Horowitz and Graf.
3 Horowitz and Graf.
4 Linda Dillow, *Calm My Anxious Heart: A Woman's Guide to Finding Contentment* (Colorado Springs: NavPress, 1998), 120.
5 Dillow, 41.

CHAPTER FOUR

1 Susie Larson, *In Over Your Head: Balance That Works When Life Doesn't* (Eugene, OR: Harvest House, 2018), Kindle.
2 Tracie Miles, *Love Life Again: Finding Joy When Life Is Hard* (Colorado Springs: David C. Cook, 2018), 47.
3 Alli Worthington, *Fierce Faith: A Woman's Guide to Fighting Fear, Wrestling Worry, and Overcoming Anxiety* (Grand Rapids, MI: Zondervan, 2017), 174.
4 Chrystal Evans Hurst, *She's Still There: Rescuing the Girl in You* (Grand Rapids, MI: Zondervan, 2017), 28.

CHAPTER FIVE

1 Shaunti Feldhahn, *The Kindness Challenge: Thirty Days to Improve Any Relationship* (Colorado Springs: Waterbrook, 2016), 17.

CHAPTER SIX

1 Maria Furlough, *Breaking the Fear Cycle: How to Find Peace for Your Anxious Heart* (Grand Rapids, MI: Revell, 2018), 47.
2 Jennie Allen, *Nothing to Prove: Why We Can Stop Trying So Hard* (New York: Waterbrook, 2017), 155.

Chapter Seven

1 Sean McDowell, "9 Important Insights about Generation Z," Josh McDowell Ministry, December 8, 2016, https://www.josh.org/9 -important-insights-generation-z/.

2 Jennifer Dukes Lee, *The Happiness Dare: Pursuing Your Heart's Deepest, Holiest, and Most Vulnerable Desire* (Carol Stream, IL: Tyndale Momentum, 2016), 13.

3 Elisabeth Elliot, *Passion and Purity: Learning to Bring Your Love Life under Christ's Control* (Grand Rapids, MI: Revell, 1984), 162–63.

Chapter Eight

1 Cigna in partnership with Ipsos, "2018 Cigna U.S. Loneliness Index," February 2018, https://www.multivu.com/players/English/8294451 -cigna-us-loneliness-survey/docs/IndexReport_1524069371598 -173525450.pdf.

2 Judith S. Wallerstein, Julia M. Lewis, and Sandra Blakeslee, *The Unexpected Legacy of Divorce: A 25-Year Landmark Study* (New York: Hyperion, 2000), 168.

3 Vocabulary.com, s.v. "afflicted," accessed May 27, 2020, https://www .vocabulary.com/dictionary/afflicted.

Chapter Nine

1 Rick Warren, *The Purpose Driven Life: What on Earth Am I Here For?* (Grand Rapids, MI: Zondervan, 2002), 17.

2 Beth Moore, *So Long Insecurity: You've Been a Bad Friend to Us* (Carol Stream, IL: Tyndale House, 2010), 104.

Chapter Ten

1 Deb Wolf, "50 Ways to Show Gratitude to the People in Your Life," *Counting My Blessings* (blog), November 16, 2016, https:// countingmyblessings.com/show-gratitude-to-people.

2 Juliana Menasce Horowitz and Nikki Graf, "Most U.S. Teens See Anxiety and Depression as a Major Problem among Their Peers," Pew Research Center, February 20, 2019, https://www.pewsocialtrends.org/2019/02/20/most-u-s-teens-see-anxiety-and-depression-as-a-major-problem-among-their-peers/.

3 Ann Voskamp, *One Thousand Gifts: A Dare to Live Fully Right Where You Are* (Grand Rapids, MI: Zondervan, 2010), 39.

CHAPTER ELEVEN

1 June Hunt, "4 Sources of Angry Inferno in the Heart," *Christian Post*, October 9, 2013, https://www.christianpost.com/news/pub-wed-4-sources-of-angry-inferno-in-the-heart-106057/.

CHAPTER TWELVE

1 Deborah Smith Pegues, *Forgive, Let Go, and Live* (Eugene, OR: Harvest House, 2015), 13.

2 R. T. Kendall, *Total Forgiveness* (Lake Mary, FL: Charisma House, 2007), 87.

CHAPTER THIRTEEN

1 Jimmy Evans, *I Am David: 10 Lessons in Greatness from Israel's Most Famous King* (Southlake, TX: Gateway, 2020), 43.

CHAPTER FOURTEEN

1 Nicki Koziarz, *Why Her? 6 Truths We Need to Hear When Measuring Up Leaves Us Falling Behind* (Nashville: B&H, 2018), Kindle.

2 Charles F. Stanley, *Landmines in the Path of the Believer: Avoiding the Hidden Dangers* (Nashville: Thomas Nelson, 2007), 82.

Chapter Fifteen

1 Micah Maddox, *Anchored In: Experience a Power-Full Life in a Problem-Filled World* (Nashville: Abingdon, 2017), Kindle.

Chapter Sixteen

1 Jaime Rosenberg, "Mental Health Issues on the Rise among Adolescents, Young Adults," *In Focus* (blog), *American Journal of Managed Care*, March 19, 2019, https://www.ajmc.com/focus-of-the-week/mental-health-issues-on-the-rise-among-adolescents-young-adults.
2 Jean Lush, *Women and Stress: Practical Ways to Manage Tension* (Grand Rapids, MI: Revell, 2008), 24.

Chapter Seventeen

1 David Kinnaman, "The Porn Phenomenon," Barna Research Group, February 5, 2016, https://www.barna.com/the-porn-phenomenon/.
2 Stephen Arterburn, Fred Stoecker, and Mike Yorkey, *Preparing Your Son for Every Man's Battle: Honest Conversations about Sexual Integrity* (Colorado Springs: Waterbrook, 2010), 181.
3 Donna Partow, *Becoming a Vessel God Can Use* (Minneapolis: Bethany House, 2004), 125.

Chapter Eighteen

1 Andrea Downey, "Rules of Attraction: A Third of Young People Say They Are Gay or Bisexual Compared to 12 Percent of Baby Boomers," *Sun*, September 27, 2017, https://www.thesun.co.uk/fabulous/4557858/a-third-of-16-22-year-olds-say-they-are-gay-or-bisexual-compared-to-88-per-cent-of-baby-boomers/.
2 Charles F. Stanley, "Moments of Weakness," In Touch Daily Devotional, One Place, June 25, 2007, https://www.oneplace.com/devotionals/in-touch-with-charles-stanley/in-touch-june-25-2007-11545170.html.
3 Pew Research Center, "Most Generations Are Indifferent about Cohabitation but Have a More Negative View of Single Motherhood,"

January 14, 2019, https://www.pewsocialtrends.org/2019/01/17/
generation-z-looks-a-lot-like-millennials-on-key-social-and-political
-issues/psdt_1-17-19_generations-10/.

4 "Sex Talk 2.0," Axis, video 3, accessed March 22, 2021, https://axis
.org/talk3.

Chapter Nineteen

1 Ben Bennett, "Resolution: Reaching a Generation with Whole-
ness," Josh McDowell Ministry, May 5, 2020, https://www.josh.org/
resolution-reaching-a-generation-with-wholeness/.

2 Monica Anderson, "A Majority of Teens Have Experienced Some Form
of Cyberbullying," Pew Research Center, September 27, 2018, https://
www.pewresearch.org/internet/2018/09/27/a-majority-of-teens-have
-experienced-some-form-of-cyberbullying/.

3 David Brooks, "The Shame Culture," *New York Times*, March 15, 2016,
https://www.nytimes.com/2016/03/15/opinion/the-shame-culture
.html.

4 Denise Pass, *Shame Off You: From Hiding to Healing* (Nashville:
Abingdon, 2019), Kindle.

Chapter Twenty

1 "Skin Picking Disorder (Excoriation)," WebMD, accessed March 22,
2021, https://www.webmd.com/mental-health/skin-picking-disorder#1.

2 "Self-Harm," *Psychology Today* (website), accessed March 22, 2021,
https://www.psychologytoday.com/us/basics/self-harm.

3 Nathan Busenitz, "The Personal Reformation of Martin Luther,"
Master's Seminary Blog, October 25, 2016, https://blog.tms.edu/the
-personal-reformation-of-martin-luther.

4 John Townsend, *Hiding from Love: How to Change the Withdrawal
Patterns That Isolate and Imprison You* (Grand Rapids, MI: Zondervan, 1996), 219.

Chapter Twenty-One

1 Patsy Clairmont, *Stained Glass Hearts: Seeing Life from a Broken Perspective* (Nashville: Thomas Nelson, 2011), 21.

2 Henry Cloud and John Townsend, *How People Grow: What the Bible Reveals about Personal Growth* (Grand Rapids, MI: Zondervan, 2001), 318.

About the Author

SARAH GERINGER is an author, speaker, podcaster, blogger, and artist. She is a member of the devotional writing teams for Proverbs 31 Ministries, A Wife Like Me, Devotable, Hope-Full Living, Kingdom Edge Magazine, and Woman 2 Woman Ministries. Her writing has also been featured on the *(in)courage* blog.

Sarah holds a bachelor of arts in English from Covenant College and a bachelor of fine arts in graphic design and illustration from Southeast Missouri State University. She is a fifth-generation resident of southeast Missouri, where she lives with her husband and three children. You can follow Sarah as she writes about finding peace in God's Word at sarahgeringer.com.